HEAT

Series 3 Number 2

Naminapu Maymuru-White
Milŋiyawuy / Milky Way 2019
Natural pigments on eucalyptus bark
Courtesy of the artist and Buku-
Larrŋgay Mulka Centre, Yirrkala, NT

This work will be included in the
exhibition *Maḏayin: Eight Decades
of Aboriginal Australian Bark
Painting from Yirrkala*, organized
by the Kluge-Ruhe Aboriginal Art
Collection of the University of
Virginia, and opening at the Hood
Museum of Art, Dartmouth College
on 3 September 2022.

HELEN OYEYEMI
LUDIC LITERATURE

Helen Oyeyemi is the author of the story collection *What Is Not Yours Is Not Yours*, along with five novels— *The Icarus Girl*; *The Opposite House*; *White Is for Witching*; *Mr Fox*; *Boy, Snow, Bird*; *Gingerbread*; and, most recently, *Peaces*. In 2013, she was named one of *Granta*'s Best Young British Novelists.

IN ONE WAY OR ANOTHER, most of my life has been a live action rendition of Rumi's 'Whoever Brought Me Here Will Have to Take Me Home', that poem of cosmic bewilderment at having somehow ended up in this world (brusquely described as a 'prison for drunks'). While it may read as if I've randomly decided to fling insults at life, I'm actually aiming for transparency here, trying to clarify the basis for the awe in which I hold the arts – which I consider the greatest gateway to acceptance of the human condition. At this point, even if the spaceship that must have brought me here finally did arrive to take me back, I'd find it very difficult to turn my back on a global civilisation that's brought forth the plays of Lorca, the Chagall ceiling of Paris's Opéra Garnier, the paintings of El Greco, orchestral compositions like Josef Suk's *Scherzo Fantastique*, the mixed mediums of William Blake and Helena Almeida, the poems of Wisława Szymborska and Gerard Manley Hopkins, TV scripts written by Kim Eun-sook, the Hong sisters and Park Ji-eun, Ildikó Enyedi's film *On Body and Soul*, Céline Sciamma's film *Portrait of a Lady on Fire*, every Wong Kar-wai film, ludic literature (more about that in a bit) and on and on and on...I could reel off lists for months at a time and still only have referred to a tiny sliver of art's astonishments.

Still, this is the respect, delight and admiration of one who is probably not one hundred per cent committed. Someone who likes human beings, but from some sort of emotional distance. This isn't a distance that induces feelings of safety or superiority or anything like that. I can't quite describe what this distance feels like. But it's always there. It's neither harmful nor helpful, and just seems to be part of the way my brain works. I can only recall a couple of instances of seeing this distance reflected in writing: the first being the behaviour of Cesminigar the tortoise, one of my favourite characters in Ahmet Hamdi Tanpinar's solid gold Cadillac of a novel, *The Time Regulation Institute*, published in 1962 and translated from Turkish by Maureen Freely and Alexander Dawe in 2014. Most descriptions of Cesminigar involve his determined attempts to scramble out of the scene. He doesn't want to be in the story. The more adamant Cesminigar is about getting out, the more likely it seems that he's not objecting to the particular story he's in – it's more that he simply *can't* be in a story. He just needs to be over there somewhere, where there are no words.

This persistent sensation of uninvolvement – and corresponding appreciation of the ability to really be present in one's own life – might be part of the reason why I resist the identification of any functional role for the arts. It's like this: when we claim that we make things up so as to have holidays from reality, or so as to strengthen our faculties of empathy, or to access higher or otherwise invisible truths or to visit other worlds, it feels like trying to put collars on creatures we were already quite naturally going about hand in hand with almost non-stop, waking and dreaming. Consider the unruly edge to any and every story – the aspect of the story that's often unavailable to its teller or creator; consider the obscurity of how a story comes to be, or begins to flow, or actually comes alive. That's the aspect that makes the purpose of stories – if there even is a purpose – impossible to evaluate. That's why it doesn't make sense to me to claim that any benefits we may have received from a made-up story are the reason the story exists. Most of us are happier when we feel we're contributing something, anything, to the greater good, and it's probably better for overall morale if the time, effort and sheer soul poured into this kind of work is matched by a concrete goal. For my part I'm not too worried about not knowing what art is really for. And I'm happy when I see and hear made-up stories being accepted entirely on their own terms as opposed to being poked and prodded for themes and such. A big step towards making more room for that to happen would be increased resistance to the temptation to send our arts, or even our sciences, out as scouts in search of the meaning of our lives. Even if a person does come across something that gets to the very heart of them, it's usually too raw to be digested by anyone other than the one who's gleaned it. The heart is a lonely hunter indeed. I can see that this set-up is daunting enough to make us scramble to do a bit of outsourcing, halving the burden of processing our own emotions by pushing the rest onto art. But then we end up in a place where it's insisted or implied that the value of art lies in its seriousness – or that without seriousness (or sombreness, poignancy or some otherwise earnest element) the invention we've just spent time with isn't art. Reading for pleasure or for fun is of course fine, but if you're reading *properly* there's got to be some profundity, or at the very least some anguish. Rather than attack this way of reading I want to show some love for writing that is entirely incompatible with the notion that there's something you should be learning from it, or any sort of cathartic message you should be receiving from it.

In his 1938 book *Homo Ludens,* the historian Johan Huizinga suggests some key characteristics of play. He observes that the players of any game are *bound by a spirit of hostility and friendship combined,* that the combative or competitive element of play is an essential component – a component accentuated by alternation and repetition; rounds and roundabouts. Huizinga states the very first characteristic of play: *it is free, is in fact freedom (entered into freely)* and later adds, almost as an aside, that *the plain fact is that play may be deadly and yet remain play.*

I want to join Huizinga and others in reaffirming that play is far from trivial, and that games are not without substance. Last year I watched a livestream of a play written by Artificial Intelligence – well, a play scripted via collaboration between a language processing algorithm and a team led by the human playwright and dramaturge David Košťák and the human linguist and robopsychologist Rudolf Rosa. So very broadly speaking we could call this ninety per cent AI authored with five per cent direct input from human scientists and the same amount from human artists. In an early scene a human asks a robot to tell him a joke. The robot replies that there is no joke. Very stern…there can be no joke here in this theatrical milestone. That in itself was enjoyable. I enjoyed the play as a whole, and felt exhilarated by its cellophane-like affect, the organisation of its ideas and the way that those ideas were linked – I wouldn't call it simplicity, but there was a lightness with which the dialogue and scenarios were connected that allowed the entire body of this hourlong play to walk on its fingertips. A somewhat roguish energy shone through on the part of the director, Daniel Hrbek, and the actors juggled the material with charisma. It was all very compelling, and had I not known that the play was in part a demonstration that AI is able to produce work that a drama fan can appreciate, I wonder what I would have given as the main reason for feeling as engaged as I did. But we can talk about the production some other time. Back to the part of the AI play where the pesky human keeps asking the robot to make him laugh. After repeatedly insisting that 'there is no joke', the robot gives in to the human's request and unleashes his best quip: *When you are dead, and your children are dead, and their children are dead, and their children's children are dead, and their children's children's children are dead, I will still be alive.*

I still can't decide if that successfully removed all playfulness from that scene, or if it heightened the unruliness of the exchange. Play antagonism or sustained refusal to play? I found some hope in that ambiguity, and in the offering of it. Hope that there is a spirit of play still afoot in at least some of the stories being made up nowadays.

By no means does it have to be all frolics all the time – any one reader is a lot of people, and variety is the only way to keep all the readers within a reader happy. Some examples from piles of books in a Prague flat: when reading a Mariana Enríquez story I no longer care about frolics – there are so many other things going on. Han Kang's writing doesn't really play around either, nor does Rachel Cusk's, nor Anita Brookner's nor Kelly Link's. My rapturous response to the writers mentioned is all about one of them being an exquisite technician, another being a ruthless manifester, one wielding bladelike prose, and then the others combining all three! Setting out in yet other directions that are neither grave nor carefree, I arrive at Diana Athill's writing, Ali Smith's, José Saramago's, Robert Walser's. And then there's Yoko Tawada's writing, and Dubravka Ugrešić's. There's Witold Gombrowicz, Anne Carson, Daniil Kharms, Heather O'Neill, Jesse Ball and others I read for thrills, but again, thrills that are quite distinct from the electrical wriggle that animates writing that's at play. Kharms and Gombrowicz, two authors whose writing personas almost completely oppose each other, do have one thing in common: their stories sometimes give a strong impression of Ludic League athletes. But to my mind the playfulness is a transient effect. The humour is there, as is the combative spark – either as subtext or more explicit confrontation, the narrative equivalent of having sand kicked in your face. These are stories you go towards; they'll never chase you. So I say they're not playing. I'll share a much-loved passage, though; it's from the final paragraph of Gombrowicz's introduction to his 1937 novel, *Ferdydurke*, translated from the Polish by Eric Mosbacher, a masterclass in introductions that are tongue-in-cheek yet simultaneously not really joking: *At worst the book will pass unnoticed, but friends and acquaintances when they meet me will certainly feel under an obligation to say to me the sort of thing that is always said when an author publishes a book. I should like to ask them to do nothing of the sort. No, let them say nothing, because, as a result of all sorts of falsifications, the social situation of the so-called 'artist' in our times has become so pretentious that whatever can be said in such circumstances sounds false, and the more sincerity and simplicity you put into your 'I enjoyed it enormously' or 'I like it very much indeed', the more shameful it is for him and for you. I therefore beg you to keep silent. Keep silent in hope of a better future. For the time being – if you wish to let me know that the book pleased you – when you see me simply touch your right ear. If you touch your left ear, I shall know that you didn't like it, and if you touch your nose it will mean that you are not sure...then we shall avoid uncomfortable and even ridiculous situations and understand each other in silence. My greetings to all.*

I want to stick up for stories that play because they tend to be the ones that we're quickest to lose patience with; since they don't attempt to draw us in with sorrows and profundities, they're meant to be relaxing, apparently. I suspect ludic tales may be the ones most abruptly dropped for not behaving as toys ought. We'll drop the book without a word, but if something does have to be said about it – if a friend insists on knowing why we didn't keep reading, for instance – we'll say a book engaged the mind without engaging the heart: a critical formula that may help us avoid confessing that the heartlessness was ours, or that we felt mocked by the authorial voice, the idiosyncrasies of the text, the sequencing of events, the footnotes, all of it, really.

I don't come across stories that play as much as I used to and want to, and I very much hope that we're not running out of them. Perhaps they're retreating from the contemporary English-language book world. Does this language of ours somehow inhibit the conception of something as gorgeous and as formally frustrating as Éric Chevillard's *The Author and Me*, a novel-length sentence most wilfully punctuated so as to remain readable without the use of full stops? That one was written in 2012, and Jordan Stump's English translation, published in 2014, is as much of a feat as the novel itself. Without trying to pigeonhole Sabrina Orah Mark's writing – the play aspect is not the only part that's remarkable about it – I'll mention her short story collection *Wild Milk* as the only English-language option I can think of at the moment when it comes to fiction that pulses with the spirit of play. This rowdiness is present in the author's poetry, too, and the seeming effortlessness with which she pulls that current across mediums certainly makes a non-poet wistful. Let's have some more!

I hesitate before asking that we take a bit more time to think aloud about ludic literature. Past the age of eighteen I avoided the formal study of literature despite an interest in canon and in tradition. I didn't quite trust myself not to fall into a mindset where the rules of this type of story and that type of story would become so firmly fixed that I would almost automatically be prevented from reading or writing anything fresh and free-floating. Identifying characteristics of stories that play is bothersome in that very same vein. Having cracked the spines of so many different and equally wonderful styles and types of fiction and identified a potential decrease in contemporary tales that play, am I now seeking to increase the quota so we can have the same ratios as there were in, say, the twentieth century? Even if that is the mindset that's driving these thoughts, the joke would be on me. If there's any type of story that could never be identified from the portrait on a wanted poster, a story that plays is probably it. Not seeing the game coming could well be part of the MO. And the invitation is to participate in a contest that doesn't rely on the foreseeability, or even the possibility, of conclusion, but on a back and forth of impressions, ideas, doubts and certainties that call upon as many of our literacies as possible and has us reading all along the breadth and depth of our unexpectedly divided and even more surprisingly united selves. As a side effect, notions of winning and loss get scrambled like eggs in a hot frying pan.

I didn't read Barbara Wright's sleek and sparkly 1958 translation of Raymond Queneau's 1947 book *Exercises in Style* until I was in my early thirties. I have the good fortune of being friends with the Estonian writer Indrek Koff, and in 2018 I discovered with much glee that, aside from also being a publisher of children's books, he's a talented comic actor and quite a splendid trumpeter as well – skills he makes the most of as part of a performance troupe that adapted and performed some of the chapters of Queneau's *Exercises in Style* in a chapel in Tallinn. The show was such a riotous enchantment that I got the gist of it all despite not understanding a word of Estonian. And though it's true that the performers, adapters of the text and the audience were the key influence that night, when I opened the book, it felt as familiar as it did avant-garde. More than that, Queneau's high-kicking parade of ultra-short stories – each one using a different method of recounting the same altercation spotted on a Paris bus – felt like a benevolent gesture. Possibly one of the most benevolent gestures a writer can make towards a member of the masses. Ninety-nine versions of the same story, and not a single repetition! That's so loving. Not to mention a tiny bit vicious. I didn't understand – or even make much of a connection with all ninety-nine of the Exercises in Style. The entries that drew on the properties of an official letter, of dreams, plot twists, class consciousness, reported speech, doubtful neutrality, over confident neutrality, hesitant witness, outright biased witness – those versions won me over immediately. Others – the entry related via negatives, the animist entry, the philosophical entry, the double entry entry, among many others, turned my reading experience into one of curious aversions and affinities, interpretive barriers to leap over, knock down, go around or even creep under. Creeping under barriers is OK; why be unnecessarily prideful when you can be shrewd? I'll quote the deathless Jára Cimrman, The Greatest Czech, captured on camera in the 1983 film *Jára Cimrman, Lying, Sleeping* as he advises school children unsure as to how to climb a tricky fence without looking weak in front of each other: *Children, in your life you will have to face obstacles. Tyrš says: 'Jump, climb, but never ever bend down' but I say: 'You may bend down too, but then you must straighten up again!'* I was not fond of each and every one of the ninety-nine Exercises in Style, but without exactly that number of entries, I wouldn't have glimpsed fiction's frankly miraculous absence of limits – and here I refer to the ways and means of transmitting a story as well as to the ways and means of receiving it.

I've heard football described as The Beautiful Game, but reading fiction that plays is the most beautiful game of all. An activity that asks a lot of you; much more than you were aware of even possessing. As you read, your pockets are unstitched and the ludic story pulls endless strings of smoked sausage out of it – or bars of gold, if you're vegetarian. But there is no defeat scenario; the story is a game, not a battle. That said: it isn't as if the game or games played in ludic fiction are necessarily pleasurable, or particularly humorous – that isn't what drives your willingness to subject yourself to its rules. I'm thinking of Ágota Kristóf's 1986 novel, *The Notebook*, a book so hard – I don't mean difficult hard, but diamond hard – that if you shift focus as you hopscotch across the grid of chapters, you could fall and break your mind on a page. Which page? Literally any page. If you've read it, I think you know exactly what I mean. If you haven't read it, please do, but I'm asking you to be careful and try to set aside six to seven hours on a day when you don't have anything else scheduled. The book was written in French and translated by Alan Sheridan into an English with an understated and fascinating throb to it, each chapter a link in a magma chain. This notebook, probably less famous than the bestselling love story, is only 167 pages long and feels much shorter than that – I think adrenaline is a factor. The twin protagonists are young enough to have milk teeth (later shattered when they're beaten during an interrogation) but they're studying the rules of life in wartime, and they are not to be sidetracked, fobbed off, or trifled with. When invited to participate in some game or other, these two answer: *We never play. We work and study.* The boys are only really dangerous to the one person in the story they catch trying to increase somebody else's truly abject suffering for their own enjoyment. This doesn't make the boys' dangerousness any easier to navigate; the character in question isn't even aware of her transgression, but the boys are aware, and so, reader, are you.

The vastness of fiction's playground (and the seeming abundance of slides and ladders) makes it possible for the reader of ludic literature to flee the corner inhabited by the kids who don't play and crash into the hall of King Arthur for all the wonder of Camelot on New Year's Day. Just in time to witness the beginning of a yearlong game that places itself on some borderline between a deeply erotic puzzle and a mystical riddle, the challenge of the Green Knight who will accept one colossal injury from anyone who dares to strike him, as long as that person is prepared to visit him and receive exactly the same injury in twelve months' time. Then from fourteenth-century England we can hula hoop over to nineteenth-century Norway and play tag with Peer Gynt as he runs this way and that, trying on the persona of a bride-abducting rascal, a hill troll, a morally bankrupt businessman, a desert prophet, a liar, a psychiatrist's assistant and a legend...but after a certain point the Gyntish one refuses to be spied on any longer, and pushes us down a mountainside, where there is no reindeer steed to spring across the abyss with us this time. Instead the reader of ludic literature falls into the lap of quite another book, a seduction simultaneously more intimate and abstract than the taut and unspeakable anticipation that runs through the tale of Gawain and the Green Knight. This other book was first published in Italy in 1979, and begins in a manner that makes you feel you're not going to have any difficulty standing aloof from it:

[1]
You are about to begin reading Italo Calvino's new novel, *If on a winter's night a traveller.*

Oh, really? Come on, you scoff. (Well, I did, at first.) But it's too late. The game is very, very, very much afoot.

PIP ADAM
UNLOCK TO RIDE

Pip Adam is the author of three novels: *Nothing to See*, *The New Animals*, which won the Acorn Foundation Prize for Fiction, and *I'm Working on a Building*. Her short story collection, *Everything We Hoped For*, won the NZSA Hubert Church Best First Book Award for Fiction.

IN HINDSIGHT, I probably heard the first ones but ignored them. They were probably background to whatever was going on in my foreground and I brushed them off. Maybe it was the microwave, maybe it was a notification on my phone. A hidden box left unchecked, something I'd lost interest in, was maybe still paying for. They were sudden noises. When there were only a few of them, at the start, the dingdingding or the chugga-chug was here and then gone before it fully registered.

The flat was not cheap and not really a flat. I was staying in the wide-open space of a coffee roastery. I wanted to say it was on the outskirts of town. That I stayed in a studio space on the outskirts of town. But when I tried it out the first few times it sounded terrible. I wanted it to sound like I was a cowboy of some sort but it came off sounding like I was a real estate agent. It was hot in the summer and freezing in the winter and twenty-seven other people lived there.

The roastery was a cover for the accommodation rort our landlord was pulling. The whole warehouse was divided with heavy curtains into small rectangular spaces where we all slept in single beds. Every space looked the same and it was hard to tell them apart. Our landlord called them pods but it was more like a battery. At least once a week I would walk into the wrong pod and lie down on the wrong bed. I bought a pillowcase with a small kitten and a butterfly on it. This worked for a couple of days but then someone stole the pillowcase. When I located it the next night I was, again, in the wrong pod.

'I think this is mine,' I said to Duncan, after he told me to get out of his pod.

'I don't think so,' he said.

'Okay,' I said and left, spending about fifteen minutes peeking through the gaps in curtains until I found the bed without a pillowcase.

Above all, peace was important. None of us had anywhere else to go. Every house in the city was full. Every garage, every car, under every bridge. There wasn't a single place left to stay. It was Bethlehem as far as the eye could see.

In hindsight, it's little wonder I didn't hear them to start off with. Twenty-seven people make a lot of noise, even when they're sleeping – especially when they're sleeping. And the e-scooters didn't all come at once.

Earlier in the year, I had gone to my parents for dinner and my father was reading his phone. My mother and father had worked hard and were older so there were only seven other people living in the rugby clubrooms they rented. It was a nice place. Someone had put up screens like people used to have in offices, when people used to have offices, so there were no curtains and there was more space, and people decorated. Occasionally, I'd be visiting and someone would come round the edge of one of the screens, see my parents and say, 'Oh sorry.' But it was a very rare occurrence.

'What about these electronic scooters,' my father had said, not lifting his head from his phone. My mother had a bluetooth headset on, so I knew he wasn't talking to her.

'Oh,' I said.

'You rent them,' he said. 'On your phone.'

'Cool,' I said.

'To make short trips.'

My father drove people around and they would pay a company money and the company would pay him a small amount of this money. He would find out who to pick up and where, from his phone which sat in a frame clipped into the air conditioning vent of their family car. Sometimes he would find himself a long way from the rugby clubrooms where he lived and he wouldn't want to drive home without a paying job so he would park the car and wait, sometimes on the side of the road, sometimes in a car park, and read his phone. When I was small he told me about the illuminati. When I was seventeen he tried to talk me into buying a seat on an aeroplane that didn't exist and was in fact a pyramid scheme but I didn't have the $100 it cost, so he asked me to ask the other hairdressers at my work. This was before the hairdressing salon was converted into an aged care facility.

My father loved his phone. He often said young people loved their phones too much, but my father loved his phone more than anyone I knew. He also drove food to people's doors and sometimes someone would ask him to pick up something else – a jacket someone had left at a party, or a pair of shoes, or a document that had been signed by someone and needed to be signed by someone else. Sometimes people would bring their pets in his car to travel the short trip to their vet. I could see his concern.

Our city is a hilly city. Like San Francisco where the scooters had come from – where everything came from. I said that. That we lived in a hilly city. And my father said, 'It's of no concern to me,' because whenever my father is scared he says brave things that are often also aggressive. My father would fight the scooters with his bare hands if they so much as tried to take the food to people's doors or the documents, and if he saw someone on one, he would smack them in the face, carry their unconscious body to the door of his white Prius and drive them to where he thought they wanted to go. A machine had taken his job at the large warehouse, which was now student accommodation, and he would have fought the machine too if they hadn't taken his swipe card off him as he left on his last day. But now the robot that picked things off the shelves was out of a job as well. 'If you wait long enough,' he said, as if he was reading my mind. 'It all comes around.'

'Oh,' I said. 'Cool.'

My mother was ordering dinner then on her phone, still talking on her headset. Asking someone if they had tried changing the password for their router. Someone would drive our food in their Prius to us. Not my father. My father was having a night off, because I was visiting for dinner. But I could tell, it was hard for him to be paying someone else to bring him our food.

The thing with the scooters was they were quiet when they were moving. When I first came into contact with them it was as they sped past me on the footpath – silently. I was not the least clumsy person I knew or the luckiest. My mother had told me when I was young that what she had really wanted was an abortion but it was impossible. She only told me once and I'm sure if I asked her again, now say, she would deny it but this comment became my core narrative – my origin story – and I spent life with a very real sense that at any moment and in a snap or some other split-second sound I would simply cease to exist. The rest of the world would be unchanged. No one would remember me, because instead of disappearing, I would have never existed. Some days this made me sad, but some days, like the day Duncan took the pillowcase with the kitten then denied it was mine, the thought – the not existing – felt like something to really aspire to. This was the soup of my subconscious. The river that ran through me, almost unnoticeable, like a stream deep under rock, and I often wondered when I wasn't sleeping if this was the cause of my constantly being in danger. I never saw another person suffer the close calls and near misses I experienced with the scooters. When they first arrived it was as if they lay in wait, just as I was overtaking another pedestrian on the clogged footpaths, or stepping round something, they would speed by – silent. But, like most things, this was wishful thinking. Soon, and in direct proportion to me looking for it, I saw more and more people jumping out of the way, shouting, and even a few being hit.

'Should they be on the road?' Adelle asked one day. We worked in a cat grooming salon and maybe she was right but I shrugged like I didn't have an opinion and probably I didn't.

Over the months there were more and more. Another company started and then another and before long it felt like everyone had their faith in the electric scooters, and that was when I started hearing them. One night, at the warehouse, the only bed I could find was against the wall of the roastery. It was freezing because the wall was tin-thin and outside was the cold, night air. I couldn't sleep, or wouldn't, because I knew someone would be along any minute to tell me I was in their bed and I would have to hunt and peck for a new place to sleep.

I think I heard the van first, but a van wasn't much, the roastery was in an industrial area and there were always vans. But then the van stopped, a gate opened, and the door of the van slid open and then I heard it, the honking and beep and then the quiet calm voice, that sounded a bit like my mother, saying, 'Please unlock to ride.' I listened as they pulled several more of the scooters out of the van, rode them a short distance inside the gate and let them fall onto what sounded like a very small but already existing pile of scooters that had already been dropped off which I had never noticed. One after another. Then the van left and it was just the scooters clicking and buzzing. Asking each other to unlock to ride. In the chatter I fell deeply asleep.

My phone alarm woke me up and as I turned it off, the honking and the chime was still there. Over the sound of the birds, the hum of the motorway falling into line with it. Like a sound bed, like it was the new sound bed of our roastery and I said, 'Good morning,' to the scooters without thinking. The service industry will do that to you.

The bathroom was busy. We jockeyed for space at the mirrors and leaned in and over each other to spit the toothpaste from our mouths. The noise of us was loud, bouncing off the concrete walls of what had surely been designed for three people at a time, maybe four. I listened hard for the scooters but the bathroom was on the other side of the warehouse and I couldn't hear them at all.

It was cold outside. I pulled my hat down over my ears. It was pointless, my glasses formed a gap and the wind blew in, so did the sound of the scooters. Each morning, the few of us who had jobs that couldn't be done from home walked with purpose to the bus stop or to the train. As the others walked past, I stood still and turned back towards the roastery trying to work out where I'd slept that night. Trying to work out which was the other side of the wall I had leaned on. Then I realised I could simply walk around the building until I found them, so I did.

I walked back to the door of the roastery and set off to the left. It wasn't long before I hit a large fence with a container on the other side of it. The sound of the scooters was further away, so I turned back and walked towards it until I hit another fence with barrels piled against it. I looked behind me but there was no one there so I searched for a gap in the barrels to look through and found one. I needed to lean way to the right, rest my head hard into the wall of the roastery, but through it I could see them – maybe fifty scooters piled up, lights flashing, chattering.

As I watched trucks started arriving with more and more scooters. Instead of riding them gently to the pile these drivers threw them from a distance. Sometimes as they flew the scooters would call out, still in the calm voice, 'Please, unlock to ride.' As they landed they would honk – chugga-chug – angry and helpless as they lay in the pile, prompting more cries from the scooters they had hit or displaced. By lunchtime there were about a hundred of them and the trucks kept coming throughout the afternoon.

Probably from the moment I heard the first van, I knew I was going to climb the fence and visit them. The trucks stopped around two in the morning. I'd been there all day curled up now beside the fence listening. As they lost their charge the earliest ones to arrive slowed down adding an alto, then a tenor, then a bass, to the conversation that never fully lifted into song despite the three-note melody of the tones that almost resolved into something like striking clock bells. I was cold by 2 a.m., tired and I hadn't eaten so it sounded more and more like they were calling me. The fence seemed somehow lower and, as I listened to the last truck leave, I felt strong and like if I could get to them I would be home in some kind of way I had never fully felt.

So I scaled the fence, not easily, not with any kind of grace. Once over I climbed awkwardly down the barrels and stepped onto the pile of scooters causing several of them to greet me with a honk which, like my father, sounded aggressive but was probably prompted by love. Walking across them was difficult. They shifted under my step and some of them tried to capture me by the ankle, they wanted me to stay that badly, but I was bound for the highest point of the pile where I could look out over them all. At the top an overwhelming tiredness came over me and I clicked and chimed and they clicked and chimed back at me as I lay down and sunk into the pile. The scooters readjusted themselves to nurse me deep within their honk and beep.

SAMUEL WAGAN WATSON
MIN-MIN

Samuel Wagan Watson is an award-winning Indigenous poet and professional raconteur. He is the author of five collection of poems, including *Smoke Encrypted Whispers*, which won the NSW Premier's Literary Award for the Book of the Year and the Kenneth Slessor Prize for Poetry. In 2018, he was the recipient of the Patrick White Literary Award for his significant contribution to Australian literature.

DAVID HAD NO IDEA what was bearing down on him. He was out in a field, somewhere. Just a flat, seemingly void expanse. Suddenly, an orb so brilliant appeared in the landscape and began closing in on the Aboriginal man. He was like an *animal* caught in the headlight of something unstoppable.

David's options were limited. Panic was about to set in. He wore light trousers and a buttoned-up shirt. He had shoes on. Whatever the light was it provided him with a means to escape. Shoes allowed him to negotiate the terrain. He bolted, his body casting crazed silhouettes that led the way. Starlight. Shrubs. Tussocks of grass. A soft, sandy floor to run upon.

Pain overtook his legs. He felt the prickly leaves of all kinds of scrub rip across his calves. The white flare of the mysterious revenant and its static being was almost on top of him. He could feel an energy tickle the short hairs on his scalp.

The fuck is this?! He wasn't an athletic person. Nor was he aggressive. This situation made no sense. Adrenalin injected him. He was determined to stay unharmed. He was yet to conclude that his life was in peril. All he needed was a solution, or a bargaining chip.

There weren't any streetlights or structures on the horizon. He dreaded the consequence of having nowhere to run to and nowhere to hide.

LEAVE ME ALONE!

An incessant *buzzzz* was now within reach of him and he felt some type of impact was imminent. He ran, throwing his arms about. If he was yelling it was because he had little control over his voice. The weight of his body, the flailing of his limbs resulted in a violent crash, arms and legs, and tumbling torso. He caught a glimpse of his convulsing form; it cast shapes of lunacy into the afterglow.

The luminosity of the object was spectacular! It hovered for seconds above the mess of David's collapse. Then, unbelievably, the phosphorescence died, without a trace of residue. His eyes took longer to recover, the effects were as intense as a solar flare.

He rolled into a foetal position then lay on his back. The stars twinkled above him. He exhaled his terror. He gulped silently, his heart beating against his chest. He grasped himself tightly. The orb had burnt its imagery into his conscience. Would anyone believe him? Could he believe it? Any proof of what had just occurred disappeared into a fading whisp of smoke.

Looking around him, small specks of flash blind-danced in his eyes. Rubbing his eyes gave him little relief. Every time he blinked the inside of his lids reflected magnesium glimmers.

He rolled his neck. His body began imagining the pain it was recovering from. He was embraced by darkness. And it quickly became apparent that not a cricket nor any other living creature disrupted the peace in David's vicinity. He remained prone, tenderly moving his lumbar region, testing whether or not he was the victim of a delayed spinal injury.

He allowed himself a gentle whisper, 'What...was that?'

He lay, half comatose by brain chemistry and his own inability to solve what had happened. He lifted himself somewhat, his aching elbows allowing him a small elevation above his surroundings.

Where the fu—?

Amid the still dark, where not even a breeze dared to meander, the forty-year-old Aboriginal man fell back into the earth. If he was anywhere, he was a world away from where he should have been.

34

The ground faulted, but as silently as the surrounding night. David's body was swallowed in an instant depression, so chimerical it was, that his last glimpse of the orbiting heaven was coldly nefarious in its wonder.

The insanity of the soil shared witness to a hundred dark, festering hands, tearing at the man's helpless body, limpid as he was snatched; pulled under by an unknown entity, the cavity coughing a blasting cloud of dust. Evil-smelling digits wriggling back into the hellish frenzy from where they'd rapidly emerged.

LUKE CARMAN
SIT DOWN YOUNG STRANGER

Luke Carman's debut story collection, *An Elegant Young Man*, won the 2014 NSW Premier's New Writing Award and was shortlisted for the ALS Gold Medal, the Steele Rudd Short Story Prize and the Readings New Writing Award. His second collection of stories, *An Ordinary Ecstasy*, is forthcoming in July.

SUNSET HUNG OVER THE MOUNTAINS when Liam stepped off the carriage into the sting of Katoomba's twilight, hoisting his guitar case over the gap and following the evening rush of strangers in black coats and scarves down the station stairs. An electric schedule hanging from the station's awning announced the time in blinking yellow digits, an hour left before the opening, enough time to settle the nerves at a pub up the street, not enough time to become so settled the night's performance would suffer.

A sprawl of graffiti on the walls of the tunnel leading from the station out towards the footpath read 'I've done me self a mischief'. What this meant, Liam couldn't say, but it struck him the phrase might serve as a title, or a lyric that could open into melody. He let that possibility flicker inside the dusky interior plane from which all his songs had come, but nothing stuck in this instance, and all thought of the phrase was forgotten when his eyes fell upon a poster pasted outside the tunnel's arch. The poster read *Blut und Märchen – an exhibition by the artist Annie Aver-Mann*. Dominating the poster's arrangement was the print of a painting which depicted a pale, thin girl with long black braids covering her nakedness, standing in the clearing of a leafless forest like something from a fairytale. Along with the title of the exhibition, the advertisement promised a 'free acoustic performance by Liam Henley'. The sight of his name in print was still a giddying thrill, even on this minor scale, disturbing though to see it associated with the haunting figure portrayed in Annie's art.

'I need new friends,' Liam whispered, and looking into that painted face with its alarming dark eyes, he made the sign of the cross, 'father, son, holy spirit', and kissed his own right hand to seal the prayer, as he had done since childhood.

On the corner by the station there was an old colonial bank building which had been converted into a pub, with a lone security guard out front in a full-length leather coat that only a large, serious man could wear without a hint of theatre. The guard nodded, rubbing gloved hands together as he did so, and nudged open the door with his elbow, giving a sideways glance at the coffin-shaped guitar case Liam was dragging up the steps behind him. The case was cornball, a relic from his youthful heavy metal affectations, but its ugliness helped belie the quality of the rare guitar inside it, made it safer to travel without the threat of being rolled. Now that his name and face meant something to the world, care must be taken; there was always a want for getting one over those who'd made themselves known in this country.

Inside the pub, the patrons were bunched in mounds of coats and jackets on stools at plank-wood tables fastened to wine barrels. Antique lamps with petal rims gave a brazier glow to the bar, and Liam mistook the warm amber light for an open fire somewhere just out of view. A staircase wound its way up to a second floor, behind the bar, which led up to the hotel proper, and from above he could hear the faintest creak of floorboards over the racket and the revelry.

The ruddy scene reminded Liam of the residency he'd undertaken in the English county of Kent, three years ago, and a flood of memories came upon him of that time abroad. The tour had been his making as a musician worthy of the brand. He'd been a fine expat tourist too; had taken time off to see the gold wings of Queen Victoria's statue, high above the gates of Buckingham Palace, and he'd watched the great mechanism of the London

Eye, wheeling slowly above the thorny striations of the Houses of Parliament. Liam saw most of London like this: from the open top of a double-decker bus painted in the colours of the Union Jack, with the cockney accent of the tour guide still clear in his ears, pointing out essentials, like the Tower of London, where heads had once been mounted on spikes along the walls, and great men and women had died mad in the darkness made of lime and ragstone. Later on in the tour, Liam took time away from his proper occupation to walk the stony shores of Brighton, watching the grey-green sea foaming and roaring over acres of smooth, flat rocks; in a dank hipster brewery in Ulster he ate a bucket of mussels while England lost their World Cup hopes, and bore witness to a thousand St George flags littering the streets as the locals turned on each other in drunken disappointment. Most cherished of all these fascinations was a day spent busking for hours in the pollen-thick parks of Notting Hill, where his case filled with five-pound notes and white swans stretched out their pinioned wings by the ponds. In the English twilight, Liam sang Gordon Lightfoot's 'The Wreck of Edmund Fitzgerald' and Jim Croce's 'Time in a Bottle' until his fingers puckered and bled.

That memory, above all, was a treasure. A green-eyed girl in a sailor's costume, working a parlour bar in Oxford, smiled at his accent that night. 'I love the beer youse drink here,' he said to her, leaning forward against the too-loud music and the faintness of the light, his heart laced with German lager. 'I'm sure you do, that gassy piss you Aussies drink is rank.' This is English banter, Liam told himself, but for all his efforts he could not become accustomed to its sting. He recalled chatting to an Irish lad at a urinal in a club that same night, who asked, apropos nothing, what part of a woman the Aussie fancied most. They were both pissing into the urinal bowls, a red light coming in through windows frosted against the alley outside. The room stank of bleach, and an ungodly bass pulsed in from the club's speakers and pressed against his skull. Liam took in the Irishman's question, closing his eyes upon the image of a woman's bare belly as it flashed upon his imagination: she, whoever this woman was, was dancing towards him, smooth and brassy as desert dunes at daybreak. Seeing this impression, vivid in his mind, Liam replied with his eyes still closed, 'the thorax'. The Irishman zipped up his splattered jeans, stepped back from the urinal, his skin red from the alley's glow, and said, 'Well that's a word for it! You sure have a way with anatomy there, Mr Vocabulary.' Desperate for some smooth rejoinder, Liam offered, 'You know what they say: *use it or lose it!*' Already half out the door, with waves of sound irrupting into the rank toilet air, the Irishman called back over his shoulder, 'And you obviously lost it a long time ago, mate.'

It was the fault of the rustic insides of this old Katoomba pub, its polished curves like the gullet of a smoking pipe, which had brought these English transportations to mind. 'This tiny slice of England,' Liam thought, and rephrased this near aloud, 'A Slice of Little England.' Would that configuration make for a title? He wasn't convinced, but, for a moment, a line and an image together burst alive in Liam's inner-eye, he could see the construction drifting towards him through some second sight, but an uproar of excitement rode over the Dave Brubeck standard the pub was blowing through its speakers and dashed his thoughts to pieces. A large woman in a leather vest had caused the disturbance – she made a foghorn of her hands and bellowed across the room, 'Hail to thee, blithe spirit!', and a bald, red-bearded man dressed like a lumberjack closer to the bar had called back to her, 'It was an Abyssinian maid, and on her dulcimer she played!' This produced such a calamity of laughter from the entire crowd that Liam came near to covering his ears. These anachronisms rang familiar, were painful sounds, like branches scraping on glass in heavy winds, and whatever game the crowd was at with these mysterious quotations, Liam knew it not.

Most in the crowd were old, Liam saw in a survey of the laughing faces, soft and swollen for the most part, lines around their eyes when they were smiling, the skin hanging under their chins, and it was a relief to realise that whatever song he'd be playing tonight, it would not be for these old drunks and their strange quotations. Lord knows he'd played too often for these types, who were just as likely to chatter through the music as they were to sing along or clap out of time with the beat or stumble up on stage to make a show of it.

There was a brawny woman with short red hair working the bar whose tattoos ran down both her arms from her bare shoulders, and the likeness of a seahorse was inked on her left forearm. It was possible, he realised, as he leant his guitar case up against the bar beside him, a woman her age would know his face and name, now that it meant something, and so when she looked up from the glass of wine she was pouring, he waited for that flicker of recognition to leap from her eyes to his.

'What can I get you?' she asked. There was nothing in her voice but the question, though he tried a question of his own to increase his chances of being recognised, supposing that his voice might help her make an association with his face. 'Do you have pints here?' She shook her head, 'Schooners or middies.'

Liam took a schooner out to the courtyard and found the warmth inside had worsened the evening's sting, and the sun was well behind the mountains now. He sat at a bench in the beer garden and took to rolling a cigarette, hunching over it in hopes its small fire would help to kindle his spirits. Annie would be at the venue already, he knew, checking the hangings with her meticulous eye, half-cut, for sure, her wild mane of auburn hair stinking of cigarette smoke and licks of whatever she'd drunk. It amused Liam to think of Greg, the small, anodyne gallery owner who would be doing his best to deal with all the manic energy in that prodigious woman, nervous eyes darting back and forth around the corners of the little shop as Annie stomped around within its walls like a pillaging warrior Hun.

Parades of tourists unloaded from Greyhound buses pulled up by the cenotaph just outside the beer garden's gates, in bright beanies and puffed-up duffle coats that made it hard to tell where these foreigners might be from. Beneath the hanging streetlight, one man with red mittens aimed the long lens of his camera in Liam's direction, and he turned to see if there was something else behind him worthy of the shot, but there were only two teens in black hoodies, sitting at a bench at the back of the garden, near a brick wall veined with creeping vines, both looming over a phone that gave their faces a spectral shade. One of these young men, with what looked like a fish tattooed on his temple, was crying with laughter so completely his wet face was turning red. The other, stub-nosed and grinning wildly, said, 'Did you see that? Cunt's throwing whole raw chickens off a jetty!' This brought a sharp howl out of his breathless friend, who was now clutching his head as tears ran down from his eyes, and drops fell from his nose onto the screen. By the time Liam turned back around, the tourist with the camera was gone into the night.

As Liam looked about for the lost cameraman, Annie, the artist, materialised out of the misty streetlight as though appearing from backstage, tossed a pouch of tobacco onto the bench, and grabbed Liam with an embrace more suited to aikido than affection. 'Oh my God!' Annie cried, hopping backwards onto the benchtop and swinging the mass of her hair away from her face to re-light an extinguished cigarette. 'How are you?' she asked with the smoke between her lips, the stink of sweetened rum cutting through the fog of her heavy breathing. 'Let me get you a beer,' Liam answered, having finished his own and unready to withstand the artist's energies sober.

By the time Liam returned Annie was lighting another smoke, and there was a small stack of posters, just like the one he'd seen outside the tunnel advertising the night's proceedings, laid out beside her on the bench. The central feature of these posters was that same haunted print of the exhibition's titular painting, *Blut und Märchen*, the girl whose penetrating eyes Annie had painted, now looking up at Liam in arresting multitudes.

'So c'mon! What's it like to be famous?' Annie asked. Liam tried to laugh the question away, but Annie pressed it. 'Seriously!' she said. 'If I hear that song of yours on the radio one more time I'm going to drive a forklift through a fucking wall. Makes me sick hearing your voice when I'm at work, with overalls on and all.' She put on a sibilant sing-song voice and recited the lyrics: *the taste of my true lover gone!*

'You can't surely begrudge me my fifteen minutes.' Liam said, half to make her stop, and then to ask, sincerely, 'Why? The song doesn't meet your approval?'

Annie winced and took down half the beer he'd brought her.

'It's a beautiful bit of bedside poetry,' Annie answered. 'It's also the cringiest hipster drool I've heard my entire life. I always said you should have stuck to being a poet, not tried to become Gotye. But don't get me wrong, I still want you to sing it tonight, aye? No one knows any of your other songs, there'll be a riot if you don't give 'em the hit.'

'A fine critic you are,' Liam smiled, only lightly forced, and reached into his tobacco bag to fill some paper, 'Anyway, tonight's about your arty-farty fan-service, not mine. Are you ready for the cavalcade of adoration you're about to be swept away by? Greg's gonna make you out to be Katoomba's answer to Ben Quilty, I bet.'

'I'm foaming in the daks about it – as well you know,' Annie said. 'I hate all this fucking shit. And don't give me that look! It's easy for you. All you've gotta do is sing one lousy song – I've gotta be on fire all night. I've gotta grift.' Talk of the opening made Annie glance at her watch, an old silver thing inherited from a favourite grandfather. 'Fark! Not enough time to get pissed.' Swallowing down the rest of her beer she added, 'Can you sign this shit for me, quick.'

Liam looked over the slim stack of posters, the naked girl, lost in the dark woods, looking back at him with doleful eyes. 'Why would you want me to sign it? You're the fucking artist! These people are coming to see you!' She was deaf to this. There was no way out. Liam signed his name upon them all, though his signature looked unlike itself.

Katoomba's main street had changed since Liam had last been to town. There were Korean cafes, French 'provincial' restaurants, three American burger joints and the air smelt of pizza-smoke and charcoaled meat. Ovens glowed through the shopfronts and couples laughed and clinked their glasses outside of wine bars and whiskey joints. Both artist and musician were out of breath by the time they climbed the steep hill up to the gallery, and Liam was relieved to put his guitar case down while they made final preparations before stepping inside for the night's roles. The girl leered out at Liam from the gallery's front display, the disquieting mix of perversion and innocence looked garish in the spotlit brightness of the window. His nerves fired under a coughing fit.

'I need a cigarette,' he said.

Annie started rolling too, coughing and sighing along with him. 'Fuck, we're getting old,' she said with a long hard breath steaming into the air. Liam tried his lighter six or seven times and finally inhaled a lungful of smoke. They both looked in at the crowd and Liam could see Annie's husband, Ian, and their four brunette boys chasing each other around the place, as some older mountains folk with grey beards and champagne flutes in their hands gazed blankly at the various depictions of naked nymphs and lascivious corpses spread on darkling wastelands, and so much blood and gore and sex and fairytale as Annie's art depicted.

'Dude,' Anne said, the word odd in her mouth. 'Just wanna give you a heads-up. Jules is gonna be here.'

'Where?' Liam asked, exhaling a frail stalk of smoke.

'Here.' Annie said, nodding at the gallery.

'Jules is gonna be here? At your opening – here tonight?'

'Yeah. Just thought I'd give you the heads-up.' Annie said, looking away from Liam and in through the gallery's broad display, checking the faces in the crowd.

'Are you serious? We're about to go through the door; I'm about to play in there! How is this a fucking heads-up?' Liam swore. 'The song is *about her* for fuck's sake!'

'Dude, first, that's precisely what a "heads-up" is – imminent danger, be alert. And I didn't think she'd show, so don't get so mad! She texted me this arvo. She was the model for some of the paintings – the title painting! That's her in the window there – and on the posters! I had to invite her. You gotta respect your models, dude.' Anne gave an apologetic frown, looking at Liam's mortified state, slapped him on the back, flicked her spent smoke into the street and pushed on into the gallery. 'Look at these filth wizards!' She said in a booming voice, hugging a group of dark-haired men with wiry beards, and chains hanging from the pockets of their jeans, and the tall pale women with dyed hair and tattoos who ran over to get in on the hugs and kisses as the gallery door eased itself shut.

'I need another smoke,' Liam said to no one at all, his bent cigarette still lit and half inhaled. For a moment, despite the busy evening sounds of laughter and conversation, and the distant din of rock music coming from the RSL down the street, the only people in sight seemed to be the crowd on the other side of the gallery's glass. Annie was moving amongst them now, stomping between each clique of attendees cramped into the small bright space. Liam watched Annie circulating by the paintings, pointing out their implications, clinking champagne glasses and hugging person after person, her mass of hair flinging into their faces and knocking capers off their salmon canapés. Jules must be among their number, he knew it, though he couldn't see her in the crowd. Liam's throat was dry, and he began, instead, to see her face assembling itself in his mind's eye, a strange intrusion of panic and memory. He tried to shake the impression but his gaze fell on the painting hanging in the window. It was obvious now that Jules had been the model – the dark hair and shining eyes, her thin, curling smile and dimpled chin. How could he not have known her face the moment he first saw the poster outside the station, when his first glimpse of her in life seemed to renew its impression each time he closed his eyes at the end of the day, or stood silent and alone on an empty street corner, or sat on a train winding its way up into the mountains with a guitar case by his side, staring into the setting distance? It had been a cold night down on the Canberra plains when he first saw Juliana, during one of his shows at the Folk Festival. He'd been stumbling back across the festival field towards the silent rows of tents, tripping on the ropes in the dark, looking half-collapsed in walking sleep, and the moon rolled out from behind a rush of cloud, its pale glow pinning him down like a leviathan's eye in the black firmament. In that shivering moment was his first glimpse of Jules, sitting atop a fence around the tents, her bright eyes bold in the darkness, laughing loudly at two lanky boys who were wrestling for a lighter by the camping ground gates. It had seemed like a waking dream, and when she had caught his eye in the crowd the next morning, as he played 'I Started a Joke' during a festival session titled 'When Good Covers Go Bad', he almost lost the melody, looking into the milky charm of her fixed attention. For the rest of the song, his hands moved of their own accord upon the strings, and he sang only to her, the stranger staring back at him, so that nothing beside remained. When the song was done, she pursed her lips and whistled loudly, her head tilted to the side, like curiously fey folk summoned out of the festival's strange pagan

49

pretensions, her legs crossed, holding up her arms towards him as she applauded.

Liam let the cold Katoomba air and the stage-light shine of the gallery's window transport him back into the present. There was no hope now of playing the song Liam had planned – the song that was about her *for fuck's sake*. Picking up the guitar case and pushing through into the feverish light of the gallery, Liam's mind was awhirl with recalculation: What else can be played? What songs might be sung? Nothing was there in his internal musical catalogue but flashing static and discordant snatches of inaudible confusion.

'Liam!' A small man with slicked-back black hair rushed across the polished floorboards. Greg, the gallery owner. 'I'm so glad you're here – that woman – I know she's your mate – but good grief – I mean really – she puts me in a state! And we're about to start – how can we set you up? Is it just the one song? Are you sure?' Greg put his hand on Liam's back as he asked these questions, the small man's large eyes darting around the gallery as though he were an intruder in his own habitat. Liam answered none of his questions, which seemed to reassure Greg as he led the way towards a stool and a microphone in the far corner of the gallery. A gaunt bald woman was setting up the sound system and she nodded indifferently at the two men on their approach. Greg took his hand off Liam's back and wandered away, still asking questions without answers. The interlude had been enough for Liam to devise a new plan: he would sing a song called 'Redfern Blues' – though its original title was 'Dublin Blues' – by Guy Clark, an American folk singer. The song was one of the covers he'd recorded to fill out his EP – obscure enough so most folks wouldn't know if they were hearing something old or new, especially if he sang it the way he'd done for the album, with local references in place of Clark's originality.

The room was so bright it made for squinting at the paintings on the walls, and Liam took in the many naked bodies and bloody cheeks. He was too nervous now to deal with them as individual objects – instead they formed a kind of enclosure, a frightening wilderness of wild-eyed women and young girls in stages of undress and damnation, shadowy elfish figures being followed by hungry wolves in the darkness between the trees. Inside this strange second world of the gallery was the crowd, an undifferentiated mass of people into which he would soon be asked to pour his music. Only after the first few chords and the amplification of his voice, would he begin to see their unique faces, intense snatches and impressions coming to him throughout the elusive moments of creation.

The tall bald woman was adjusting the cables, testing something – she asked Liam some question and he answered in an absent way, the rare guitar out of its case now and in his arms, and a strange beating of anticipation like a throbbing in his ears. There was sweat on his fingers, they felt hot and clumsy, but when he placed them on the strings, the sounds they made were right, and his hands seemed to know to position themselves. He adjusted the tuning, twisted the small pegs with unconscious calculation. The woman strode across the floorboards in loud heels and handed a microphone to Greg, who was now wearing a blue jacket and a beaming smile as he addressed the gathering, the bright lights gleaming on his oily hair.

'Good evening – thank you all for coming – a characteristically snappy Mountains eve – this is an incredible exhibit – it's my pleasure to be able to present – one of Katoomba's greatest artists –'

What the little man said bounced about the room, reverberating out of the amplification system, through skin and bone, into the empty chamber of Liam's guitar and along the strings like small electric pricks upon the tightening threads of his nerves. The same mysterious energy Liam would need to call upon in just a minute's time. Greg's voice had become a countdown to something absurd – in a matter of ineluctable moments, the crowd would turn to Liam, perched like some sweating foreign specimen pinned upon a stool, and this pinioned wreck of man would be expected to summon vibrations of the throat and the strings which are called music. No mistakes would be permissible when the fatal time came, and his voice for the entirety of the performance would be forbidden to break, to lose its tune – nor could his fingers miss their mark, his wrists and fingertips must be true to their rehearsal. What barbarism was this expectation of flawlessness! Three full minutes of foul perfection! What madness led such pressures to be thrust on persons made of flesh and blood? Liam dropped his chin into the curve of the guitar, the coolness of its body easing the flush of his cheeks. It would be insanity now to look into the crowd, though he felt their swaying eyes moving towards him, and a trace of sweat rolled from his forehead – why not tears too, he could just let them out.

'Annie is an artist we've hosted here many times – each of her showings hugely successful – people love her work – these strange, seductive and sinister apparitions appeal to us in a way – in my experience – could conceivably –'

God what a folly to aspire, however humbly, to the level of

art! Better to be a face in the crowd looking out than a fool on a stool clinging to strings like a songbird wired on a swing in a cage, to be gawked at and mocked, to lose your feathers in front of their hungry attentions! Greg was turning, looking sideways at Liam now with his darting eyes. How slick and cruel that expression was, loaded with the expectation of delivery. The eyes of a butcher bird, carrying a kind of craven desperation too, a co-conspirator's threat.

'And what makes tonight even more astonishing – as if Annie Aver-Mann's art isn't more than enough – we have the incomparable musical stylings of *Liam Henley* here to perform an acoustic track from his latest album – give him a huge round of applause – to perform his hugely popular song – I always get the damn title wrong –'

There was now no time at all, the end of Greg's next sentence led so inextricably into an impossible set of duties that for Liam the end had already begun. 'Ladies and gentlemen' – this was the cue – no sooner said than a force, like a kind of bodily possession, made him light, and when he spoke into the microphone now it was as though another spirit sat inside his body, wore his flesh as a hand wears a sock for a puppet. 'This song is dedicated to Annie Aver-Mann, artist and friend.' Where did this little speech come from? It wasn't planned but it was wise – good to celebrate Annie here – tonight being about her, not music. Some other night would come for that, a night more fit, but if someone in the crowd were to hear Liam's music tonight and decide that it was Liam Henley who was the greater artist, surely he would be blameless?

Liam's fingers took dominion, found their places on strings and frets. They knew their actions better than their master – they could not be willed to miss their mark, they knew only one way to move, the way of song. Liam's body, his arms and legs, his wrists and neck, his thumbs and thighs, felt new and vital and all that was needed from him now was to sing the lines in their order, though the room really was too bright, and the faces of the crowd so very close. Some kids in attendance were tripping over each other, talking loudly to their parents. But the possessing spirit was performing now, and the first chords rippled through the confinement of the room and the crowd was held in place by the energies of song, and the room belonged to Liam Henley, whatever the sorrowful women in those paintings had to say about it.

At the first line of the first verse, he saw Jules in the crowd. She was smiling, the same huge grin she had worn when he played to her that morning at the festival. Still, he had to sing.

Well, I wished I was in Melbourne,
in a chilly laneway bar
Drinkin' rum-and-coca-colas
And not carin' where you are.
But here I sit in Redfern,
Just rollin' cigarettes,
Holdin' back and chokin' back
The shakes with every breath.

The shock of seeing Jules cleaved its way inside him, but he stayed out of his own control, and felt he saw himself performing from a vantage outside his body – guiding the course like a breeze carries a glider through the rushing air. Halfway through the song, a baby started crying, and two of Annie's boys pulled at their mother's jeans to show her something on a phone, and Liam became conscious again of the words he was singing. He wasn't sure if he'd skipped the verses between, or played them unconsciously. The song had played itself and was already coming to an end.

Applause erupted around the gallery, and laughter as Annie put her fingers to her lips for an enormous whistle. Liam felt his face flush anew. He was looking at Jules as the applause rose and fell, and she was smiling, slowly clapping her hands. He smiled back, cool sweat rolling down his body before Annie crashed into him. 'I love you, ya filthy hipster!' She squeezed him hard and her immense hair fell about him so completely it plunged the room into darkness for a long moment – he imagined Jules' attention in that darkness.

'This filth wizard has been a mate of mine since back in the uni days! I love him! But what the fuck was that song, dude! Where was the hit?' The crowd laughed and Annie stepped into her speech, explaining all the ways her art had ended up on the canvases on the too-bright walls. 'To be honest, I'm not an intellectually aware kind of artist, if there's anything going on in these works – you'll have to explain it to me.' There were already red stickers on the walls, and Annie, a champagne flute in her hand as she spoke, flushed with triumph, became so bold and expansive that Greg began to wring his hands.

Liam busied himself with his instrument, making an elaborate ritual of packing it away while Annie talked. An instinct cautioned him not to look back at Jules, though a contrary pull to do so was wriggling in his mind like an itch. 'I want to thank my dad, Teddy Mann – there he is over there – who personally framed every painting in this exhibition.' Annie

55

stopped for a moment. Her arms fell to her sides. 'Jesus Christ!' She laughed, with tears streaming down her face. Teddy, the father, a barrel-shaped man with enormous hands and blacked fingernails stepped out from the crowd and put his arms around his daughter, his own small eyes leaking tears. 'Jesus,' Annie swore. 'I can't believe I'm crying! What a loser!' Greg tried to lead the crowd into a chorus of 'aww', but no one followed.

When at last the talk was over there was wild applause, stamping of feet and whistling – the room relaxed so thoroughly that even the brightness seemed to dim, and all returned to considerations of the paintings they had come to see, some patrons armed with little red stickers, Greg darting about to agree with whatever they were saying about whichever work they happened to be interested in.

'That was good,' Jules said, coming close from out of the crowd. 'But then, you were always a talent.' Her hair was tied back tight, her fine pale cheeks lightly reddening as she stood close.

'You haven't aged a day! You look incredible!' Liam gushed, but there was so much more to say – and the words were close to spilling out. 'You're Annie's muse, so I've discovered,' he said to her, at a loss as to where he might begin. Jules craned her neck around the room as if only just noticing versions of herself in a half-dozen frames. 'What can I say? I've acquired a knack for inspiration.' She smiled broadly when she said this, and Liam could not take his eyes off the shape of that lopsided smile – even the pattern of the teeth! He could not but think: I have kissed her mouth. He had kissed her in his dreams of late. A thin-shouldered man in a grey leather jacket stepped up and loomed into the conversation, his expression as impassive as a mannequin's.

'Liam, this is Manny.' Manny shook hands without turning his eyes from Jules as he announced, 'We really need to get going.' Jules affirmed his statement with a nod. 'Manny's a DJ – he's got a show tonight, too!' She patted Manny on the shoulder as he turned away from them both. 'It was good to see you! Sorry we have to rush off!' Liam tried to respond, but the most he could do was open his mouth and shut it again. He repeated this action twice more and had to use a hand to prevent it repeating for a third time. Jules waved goodbye as she followed Manny out the door, into the dark Katoomba street, passing the haunted version of herself hung in the gallery window, a small red circle beside it now.

Jules had left a half-empty glass of champagne on a table of canapés beneath a painting called 'Elfen in nassem Leder', which depicted several elfish women, nude but for the thinest strips of leather wrapped around their bodies. These bare figures were wading into a hot spring overlooking an autumnal woodland. It was clear that Juliana had been the model for all three of these luminous beings. Liam took her abandoned glass and sculled it, refilling it quickly from a bottle by the canapés. He swilled that glass too and repeated this action three more times.

Liam hoovered two salmon and caper canapés into his mouth and again, sculled the drink in his hand – and poured another. A man with long thinning hair wrung out in a mess of directions was now standing beside him, looking up at 'Elfen in nassem Leder'. Liam blinked at him, there was something familiar about his face. 'I know you!' he said, shocked to recognise the man's face. 'I know you, sure, I know you! You have one of those social media blogs where you go round eating burgers and kebabs. I saw you on television once! You go to Granville and eat chicken, you go to Ashfield for dumplings! You eat those giant burgers at food trucks and drink litre milkshakes with big chunks of ice-cream on the top!' The stranger looked back at Liam as though he had pulled a switchblade on him. 'Yes,' the man confessed, he was indeed the man with the food blog. 'Fuck, dude! That must be a wonderful life! You eat out three times a day, seven days a week, and every cafe and bar in the country has got to impress you, has to excite your particular fancy, or you tear their work apart with a savage review! What a bloody barrel you've got those businesses over, aye?' The man confessed it was a nice gig. 'Yeah, I'd like to go around stuffing my face all day, it must take a lot of finesse. Where did you eat this evening? You tried the waffle house? The French provincial? You give 'em a good review, gunslinger?' It was his day off, the man explained, and then excused himself and left the gallery. Liam picked up a bottle of champagne and put it to his lips. Imagine a balding food blogger buying a work of art like that! Some rotund sensualist, gazing up at half-nude elves as he strips down on his bed before the mirror! Liam felt the urge to turn the canapé table on its head and kick out the legs. Greg appeared at his shoulder, and put a hand on his back, almost patting him. 'Liam, Liam! You were so good buddy – you consider that Chandon bottle yours – it's on me – least we can do for the song – but please use a glass, okay bud? They'll take my licence away if you get too rock-and-roll!' The small man laughed and scurried away, his eyes darting back at Liam as he did so. Annie now had one arm over her father, the other on her husband, their children huddled together in the corner watching YouTube videos on the phone. There were red circles next to most of the paintings, and the crowd showed no signs of detaching from the artist's orbit. The musician looked over the room one last time, snatched up his guitar case and stumbled out into the night without a word to anyone.

It was bitterly cold but Liam's blood was ringing in his ears as he staggered down the street, passing loud couples drinking outside bars and restaurants with their glowing heaters. There was an image burning bright in Liam's mind of the afternoon he'd spent in Notting Hill, the swan-swept park where he'd played out the day with Gordon Lightfoot and Jim Croce by the gentle hills, under a wide clear sky. The stars were all out now, and the moon was high, and Notting Hill was on the other side of the world, but there was no law against busking at night – he could throw his case open right here, or outside the gallery, and sing like a troubadour. A woman in a Rastafarian hat rolled her eyes at her nose-pierced partner when Liam stumbled on a jag of the concrete footpath in front of them, almost dropping the half-empty bottle of Chandon. The decline of the street made it easy to trip, and distant rock music was coming from the RSL a few streets away. Liam remembered a park at the bottom of the hill where it would be quiet, an amphitheatre in the heart of the park where he could play.

'Kingsford Smith Memorial Park'. This was the place he was looking for, though it was darker than he had expected, and the tops of trees around the archway seemed to loom over the path circling down deep into the strange crater-like depths. By the time Liam lugged his guitar case down to the bottom pit of the empty park the Chandon was finished, and his ragged breath was pulsing steam. There was a dim lantern filled with dead insects near the amphitheatre, and the moon was hidden by the top of an old apartment beside the station. Moths made silent sweeps at the flickering lantern, and Liam placed his open guitar case underneath, so that anyone wandering down the winding path could pay their respects to his work. He slipped into the strap and held the guitar in his arms, swaying slightly. His fingers were cold and stiff, but they knew their place, and their movements gave him the nerve to play into the silence. His hands pulled his voice along, and when the song came from his lips, out into the cold, it rolled around in the wide icy night with a purity he'd never known before.

Long ago at the festival
under a wide April night
she was the girl I'd love best of all
and I dreamt about her tonight.

We walked the town for an hour
remembering the people we knew
then she took me to her tower
I climbed up her hair for the view.

In the morning she's leaving me
as all sweet dreamers will do
she was always the best of me
my sweetest dreaming come true.

She used to roll old gold cigarettes
the taste on the tip of our tongue
ten thousand years though I'll never forget
the taste of my true lover gone.

Liam played the final chords and let the song disappear into the park's indifference, a little shocked at how intensely he'd pitched the words into living air. Just for a moment, the silence that followed seemed to envelope everything. He felt the hairs rise on his skin and noticed a strange mist had gathered in the trees, so thick he couldn't quite see the lights of the houses or the streetlights near the station. Somebody was moving through the mist. A train passing through the station stirred the silence, and bats squeaking in the trees, and a possum walking unnoticed near the gate was reaching up towards the branches of a twisted tree near the park's arch. Liam's eyes were wide at the figure coming through the mist – it was Jules, her apparition summoned by his song! Liam let the guitar hang from his body and stood silent, and when Jules stepped fully out of the mist, he had to blink hard to see it wasn't her at all, but a man in a hoodie with his head bowed and his hands in his pockets. Then a second hooded figure appeared, following close behind the first. Before Liam could adjust to this transition, the hooded men were standing close to him, the first saying, 'Sick song, bro!' The man was young, with a pale puckered face and small shaded eyes, above which was tattooed something like a fish. 'Thanks,' Liam tried to say, but his voice was dry, and the word was barely audible. 'Hey. You ever seen a three-metre flatty?' Liam looked at the young man, who lit a smoke in his hands so that the flash of the lighter's wheel turned the inside of his hood into a fiery bowl. 'A what?' was the best Liam could offer in answer. There was a dull, echoing sound, like somebody dropping a rock on a hollow log.

Soon the park's mist was gone, and the bats and possums had quit, and the early morning light was purple in the sky. Lying in the grass, Liam dreamt of a large stage, his small body in its centre. 'I'm forgetting my lines!' He'd been saying, looking out at the blinding lights and the invisible crowd. When the poor show was over, he came down into the rows to meet his friends and thank them for coming, and a terrible awkwardness fell over the hall. 'I didn't know my lines,' he was explaining to someone. 'I've never known them, never!' He began to sob in his dream, and on the stage behind him he heard Orson Welles announce, 'Well, if you want a happy ending, that depends, of course, on where you stop your story.' Juliana put her hands on Liam's shoulders. 'You'll recover from this,' she said. Liam started to move. There was no stage, at all, only earth, slightly spinning. Sky and tree and wet, cold ground. When the shock subsided, Liam saw his guitar and its case were gone, and he found the strength to raise himself up onto his knees. He knelt there, making a strange choking noise, as close to laughter as the pain allowed. Up in the branches of a tree was a kookaburra, looking down at Liam, rolling its head from side to side, wondering what to make of this strange, wormy thing in the grass below.

MICHAEL FARRELL
THREE POEMS

Michael Farrell is the author of eight collections of poetry, including *Family Trees* and *I Love Poetry*, which won the 2018 Queensland Literary Award for Poetry and was shortlisted for the Kenneth Slessor Prize for Poetry. Michael also edited *Ashbery Mode*, an Australian tribute to John Ashbery.

In The Year Of Our Modernism 1922

We tend to gender our
grandparents more than we do ourselves. He dyed his
hair...she had a more serious operation. They first started
publishing things in Europe
There began to be
articles about them. They were always having rebirths –
comebacks – cleansings. Some of the language seems very
dated now (some offensively so). Did you really have a
spider tattoo, asked my cousin Deborah, seeing our
grandmother's scar one summer? We barely knew them...I
think they didn't know each other that well. They seemed
more

affectionate than our parents but were actually more literary
...self-conscious, quoting things we didn't know were quotes
It might seem arch or precious yet I think was in some way
meant as a keyhole to the past, their pasts, plural. A verbal
equivalent to the music I'd play or food I'd eat when around
them. I wasn't quoting anything I'd written, but what if I'd
become a musician or food-something? For example, saying
that her only weapon was love, or his announcing the story of
the
hand towel. When I watch movies about the 1920s I feel no
recognition. They were never married...never had anything

as creepy as a patio. I think I get my narcissism from them...
the way the colour of my skin falls away just under the cheek
What are you lot colluding about now? my parents would say

when they came to pick me up. Quite disrespectful language
now that I think of it. There would be time to unpick all their
issues later on. In the year of our modernism 1942, say. My
grandparents would never do more than give my parents
looks
They had had everything first hand or at least in a more
immediate sense than my cousins...I. They'd waved on
piers
Seen food being made for prison visits. Not that my parents

were siblings but I have to conflate this a bit to get it all into
one poem. Occasionally they get mentioned in the northern
hemisphere even now, but you'd have to go to Wikipedia to
know they were Australian. All for Empire, my grandmother
would
say, handing me a tea towel or my grandfather, handing me
an
axe. Somehow she caught on to Dead Or Alive's 'Turn
Around...Count 2 Ten' when I'd never even heard her
mention Josephine Baker or Liberace, or listen to anything
pop. It was a sketch about

their relationship. It's sad. Funny though that that song's
more recent than the one we sang camping with my parents
('Oh Yoko'). In the middle of a poem I call their names
(Norma, Harold). If
it's sad now, too, it is more loving. My grandparents lived
under a pine
tree...called needles line breaks. They lived by a river...
were visited by ducks, fisherwomen. They didn't write

anything there, as
far as I know, apart from letters which were firmly set in the
present. How much did you get for that? They might ask if
their correspondent had mentioned selling something. When

I was ten the stamps were exciting enough...now they seem
bland...kitschy. My grandfather spoke more...more in
pastiche when he became widowed. Came down the Paris
boulevards looking for a mouldy stick. Who would've
thought
the ladies would save the Jews from Pétain? Guess they
weren't so caricatural after all. They called even damper a
stick or log of bread...had cats called Salon...Mondriaan
My dad once referred to them sarcastically as Bush Parisians
Yet I think they really only passed through. What's a year in

a long life? My grandmother talked more about TB
(tuberculosis) than any
war, but I realised she was more careful than she seemed
I have her mother's portrait of her at eighteen, looking witty...
cranky, some kind of campaign in mind. She was briefly
famous for a Hemingway parody called 'Nursing a Boxer'
I found her copy of A Farewell to Arms on a shelf, looking
half-read. Later I associated him with Kirsty MacColl's
'Walking Down Madison' as if the distance from anyone's
birthplace
(Oak Park, Illinois) to that of death (Ketchum, Idaho) (or in
her
case, Croydon, UK, to Cozumel, Mexico) is 'not
that far'.

On Meeting A Retired Orange

It was in the 00s, I had a job in Melbourne for a couple of weeks, working on a story, and I suggested to my editor I might also do a profile on the titular Mr Fruit. We had arranged to meet in the lobby of his building, but then he decided upstairs would be both more comfortable and convenient. I assumed these adjectives were euphemisms. If the article needed colour, it was there for the transfer in 'call me Dirk's' apartment. But it was also distracting, looking at the gold soccer balls, the purple inflatables, and the movie posters. Dirk made us drinks while I was reminded of several dreams I'd had that week, of a book on Freud, a basement flat with a view of a record shop, a Danish that a man brought into a café in Berlin, that was a cushion for its own topping. Some of the posters featured Dirk, who'd had a brief career in LA, and had also toured the east coast doing cabaret. Have you spent any time in Western Australia? I asked, thinking this was a fairly neutral question to start us off. I had done some research of course, but there were a lot of time gaps, and Dirk had pretty much already retired by the advent of the internet. He twiddled with the clove in his cheek, as if it were a nuance adjuster of historical trauma. It turned out – off the record – the whole thing was off-off-off – that Dirk had done a support act for Fantasy Walker in Perth, it was an unofficial thing but also a cover for Fantasy's affair with a local footballer, and Fantasy was too messed up to perform, and Dirk had to take the fall in some way: was literally told by Fantasy's manager to fall off the stage. 'I'm not a stunt act,' Dirk had replied witheringly. While that was an intriguing/boring story, I was more interested in what my readers would be interested in: Hollywood and its sucking up of Australian talent, making them so popular they were like craft spokespeople, with indeterminable accents, paraded at black tie parties like weird big talking cats...But I was getting distracted by my own prejudicial thinking. 'Can you tell me about working with Quentin Tarantino, and how that came about, he read something about you somehow, and created a role based on your own life, for the movie *Salad Mayhem*?' 'Yes,' said Dirk, 'Quentin was in a Sydney café, flipping through the *Star Observer*, and got drawn into a little biographical profile about me, and created the character Orange la Grande based on it, and which I played without too much difficulty. Orange la Grande is an ex-cop drag queen with a coke habit, which she manages to kick, and who then takes down the drug cartel responsible for exporting this particular supply to the US, and falls in love with the son of a drug lord. Lots of gunfire and local music. I hinted to Quentin that there was a potential sequel to the story, and he seemed charmed by the idea. I still write to Paolo, the actor who played my romantic interest, you know.' 'Do you miss show business?' I asked. 'Oh,' he said, and his 'oh' was like a crow, making a white deposit on a cat below, 'I was never interested in the entertainment industry, really, I'm an artist. I prefer doing non-commercial projects. People associate me with the early 90s, or the late 80s, and want to keep me in one of those boxes, lined with their own restrictive notions of irony, and critique, which they can bring out at boring parties, but I never actually retired. I've been working on an opera based on 'Five Bells', it's an Australian poem from 1939, and I've been writing songs with Paolo on Skype, we're not sure of the format to present it in, or where. There is a Five Bells opera evening in Chelsfield, which used to be a village in Kent, but is now treated like a London suburb. I'm not sure how the locals feel, but I have Kentish ancestry myself, so that would be nice. Or we could do something in Pasto, where Paolo is, in Colombia. I can see the poster now, can you? We'd need some funding, of course.' 'That certainly doesn't sound commercial!' I agreed, or thought I was agreeing. Dirk narrowed – or chilled – himself towards me at that point. 'I thought it might make the basis for a Terence Davies movie.' I started looking up Terence Davies on my phone, which seemed to affront Dirk. 'Terence Davies! My God!', and then began singing a song which seemed to be called 'Different Curios' (also very pop title I thought sourly, afterward) in a kind of Barbra Streisand's 'The Way We Were' mode. 'That's what we were to each other'; 'different languages, different cultures': it seemed oddly apt, that the sequel to a Tarantino movie would be recast as a Terence Davies movie, who I remembered, when I found him online. 'Are you actually in a love relationship with Paolo?' I dared ask, as I made moves to leave. 'I'm interested in difference, not love,' said Dirk, in a mean intellectual tone. 'Love dissolves difference.'

Drag The River

A river can **be** any SHAPE or SIZE. You could **be standing**
Downstream looking upstream. You could be **standing**
Cross-stream. A river **could** be round or square. There **could**
Be anything in it. Your childhood or a song. **To** be
Narcissistic. **To** be SUBJECT-forming When that **horse** is gone
Horse or **boat** or horse-**boat**. I'm assuming There's no
Platypus with magic claws **or** bridge which falls as my **Or**
Let's say our ENEMIES arrive behind us. Choking in the
Dust of **The** bridge which aided in **the** establishment of this

Settlement. I Don't think brown-**eyed** beings are more
Like rivers...blue...Green-**eyed** people **like** seas. My cat
Has blue eyes...she is **like** NOTHING on the **planet**
Which **planet**? **That** is my own question Trying to trick me
When you've lived near a space station you'll Never
Want to live ANYWHERE else. No one knows how many
Disappeared into *Grand Theft Auto* before it was
Discontinued. I played **That** river a couple of times. When
He was Eleven **he** was Langston Hughes when **I** was eleven

I Had a different name. Hughes Went to Mexico...**had** A)
A good TIME...B) **A** bad TIME. There's Your Central
American poetry reference. I hardly even went to Orbost
When I was eleven but my parents were together. That's a
Privilege. There is a photo of me **on** a white horse. We are
Not Riding like the wind. Someone **on** Grindr says they hate
bigotry...weak types. **Some** things are more Attractive
With our glasses Off...**some** things Look more dangerous
From above. I slung my Hook over **my** Shoulder to see what

Was in the water. I saw **my** cat W Or Dub for short / long
It **was** her reflection looking at a Floating Bag which **was**
Actually medieval garb. Once I would've retrieved **It**...
Washed **it** worn it at the market. But To look nice it would
Need Hemming with something Red...perhaps
Embroidering. Are those Days gone? If So I Will have to buy
My Dub a bonnet...send **Her** out to Be A governess...
Only see **her** at Christmas when she'd Be A Different
PERSON probably. I imagine that I am a Blue-Eyed cat

Perched on my grandmother's shoulder away From The
Ducks...we're looking for treasures in the Receded
Floodwaters. That is what I would rename the House If I
Could afford it. Spend my RETIREMENT thinking **Of** carp
Fishing. Making geometric Portraits **of** the river Out of
Something. This **box** is a river. It is Called 'River **Box**'
I would silently rename the **river** Box **River**...Get caught...
Be driven from the town losing Dub...Thousands of
Dollars worth of sculpture in the PROCESS. That didn't...

Won't Happen as I'll never leave the Space station. I'm
Addicted to the radioactivity. It **gives** me Stronger
Perceptions than The romantic musings of CHILDHOOD
It **gives** me stranger pets than Dub. I wouldn't Drink the river
Water here. Students **do** Sometimes. The most daring
Thing I **do** is go out at night in a purple Schiaparelli dress as
If it's WARTIME...**all** bets are off...I once Told
Merriam-Webster that I heard the phrase '**all** Bets are off' in
My Brain but they said I must have read It SOMEWHERE

Or saw it on The TV. It's a nasty abusive Kind of
Phrase now I think about it. I **Would** prefer it If people didn't
Use it AROUND me. When I was Eleven...in Full view
Of the square river I **would** dress up as A man. To think of it!
Abuse back then was like something I'd read A Bit like
One **end** (the dark grey coarse **end**) Of a Rubber. (As in an
Eraser) or the other (smooth Slippery white) End. I
Think I mean sex not abuse. The dress is a good luck Charm
That I pass Around my friends. But the town's

Practically Empty at Night. The people who work at the space
Station do not Come out. They have **their** own bar
According to **their** Employment **Ads**. The **ads** seem very
Needy like they Really would love to have Us working
For Them I can find all the **toads** I want at The river
Toads Work at detoxifying the river which is to
Everyone's BENEFIT. I have a little **dragon** but they don't do
Anything Useful. I saw a fortune teller once who said
If I killed my **dragon**...boiled...ate it I would find LOVE...

HAPPINESS. What an awful person! I **love** my dragon
When it's There with its yellow eyes flashing like sunshine
It knows ALL About being eleven...can cough up bits
Of food in all kinds of River shapes. Even in a small empty
Town with barely any memory Of the rapes of wartime
I wouldn't go as far as the bridge dressed As a man or
Woman without a dragon on my shoulder. They're so Cute
They disarm anyone...**they** take up virtually no SPACE
Back in our box after chats with people in the river

73

REN ARCAMONE
ALLEN

Ren Arcamone is a writer from Sydney. She is a graduate of the Iowa Writers' Workshop and an alumna of the Clarion Science Fiction and Fantasy Writers' Workshop. Her work also appears in *Gulf Coast*. She lives in Iowa City, where she is at work on a short story collection and a novel.

PHIL AND I HAVE A MAKE-BELIEVE HOUSEMATE – we call him Allen. Allen is a real jerk. Allen never cleans the bathroom, leaves the fan on when no one's home, and only half-empties the dishwasher. Allen lets the laundry stay out on the line for so long that all our jeans are sun-faded, and he alone is responsible for the murder of our beloved houseplant, Fernie Sanders. He never vacuums. He never takes the dog for a walk. 'Fucking Allen,' we say, when we wake up with hangovers and the kitchen counter is splotched yellow with turmeric stains. 'Fucking typical.' Allen hides Phil's shaving cream the morning before his job interview at The Orchard, a boutique advertising agency. 'Allen!' Phil yells at the bathroom mirror. 'Allen, you bastard! Get your own bloody shaving cream!' In the end he uses mine and he leaves the house smelling of coconut, but he gets the job. On the weekend we go out for cocktails and enumerate Allen's flaws.

'Allen's from Vaucluse and he grew up with a maid. That's why he doesn't know how to do the ironing.'

'Allen went to an all boys' college and misses the days he used to shave off people's eyebrows.'

'Hmm,' I say. 'I think Allen's more sensitive than that. Allen did hazing in college, but now he says he's reformed. He's a Sensitive New Age Guy. But he's still afraid of women's periods.'

'Right. He's scared of female bosses and bisexual men.'

'Jesus. Grow up, Allen.'

'Allen tells people he read *The Game* "ironically".'

'Allen's Tinder profile is a quote from David Foster Wallace.'

'I bet he hasn't even made the bed. Fucking Allen.'

And sure enough, when we get home, gin-drunk and already regretting our Saturday brunch commitment, the bedsheets are tangled and the pillows are slumped in distant corners of the room, like victims from a bomb blast. Our dog, Archimedes, is huddled under the sheet clump and seems surprised to see us.

'Meedy!' Phil says. 'You know better! Off, come on, off!'

'Actually,' I say, coming back to the bedroom with two glasses of water. 'I actually think it is your turn to do the dishes. Will you do them tomorrow?'

'For you, Liz? Anything.' He grabs me and kisses me and water sloshes onto the floor and a little bit onto the dog. I put the glasses on the bedside and fumble with his zipper and we roll into bed, struggling out of our clothes. I bite his neck and he yelps.

'Be quiet,' I say in his ear. 'You'll wake Allen.'

In the morning we lay in bed and groan for an hour. 'Get me a Berocca,' I say.

'Get it yourself,' says Phil. 'Can I have some water? Where's that glass?'

'Where's *my* water?' I say. 'You stole them both!'

The two glasses are still filled up and sitting in the sink.

'You must have been sleepwalk-cleaning,' I say, although the rest of the house shows no evidence of this.

'Creepy move, Allen!' Phil says to the ceiling.

This is the day the spoons go missing. We don't notice it, at first. We drink bloody marys at brunch with Phil's theatre friends, and when we get home Phil takes a three-hour nap and I lie on the couch with Archimedes for TV1's Nineties Nostalgia Fest, catching half of *She's All That* and the entirety of *The Truth About Cats & Dogs*. I get up to make myself some green tea with honey. There are no spoons, not in the dishwasher or the dish rack, none hidden under the risotto-encrusted pan soaking in the sink. I stack the dishwasher, slowly. No teaspoons, dessert spoons, soup spoons, zero.

'Phil!' I yell. 'Do we *own* spoons?'

We are adults, I mean legally. We've been out of university for a year and both of us have landed full-time jobs: he in digital, me in copywriting, which is another way of saying we both work in advertising. We have money and independence and a chore roster marked out on a whiteboard that we both routinely ignore. And we throw dinner parties. We definitely own, or owned, at least for some period of time, multiple spoons.

'I'm asleep!' Phil shouts back.

We carry on with life, sans spoons. I keep meaning to go to Big W and forgetting about it, and then Phil starts stealing cutlery incrementally from the kitchen at his work, and we decide we don't actually need more than four spoons, total.

Friday night drinks at The Tipple are now a regular fixture. It's exciting to have real jobs to complain about and enough money to drink pinot gris past happy hour. We get there before the rush and secure two swivel seats at the front window so we can stare out onto the footpath at all the people with silk blouses and mortgages and opinions about the economy. 'Do you think we could pass for them?' Phil says dreamily.

'Someday.'

He clinks his glass to mine. 'Allen,' he says, 'is a wine snob.'

'Allen thinks Japanese whiskeys are overrated. But only because he read it in a men's magazine.'

We reflect. My pencil skirt is slippery on the bar stool and the sky is doing that red-gold Sydney sunset. I feel like I'm melting, but slowly and pleasantly. Phil takes a noisy wine gulp.

'Allen self-describes as "an audiophile".'

'Yes,' I say. 'And he has the complete discography of The National memorised.'

'Wait!' says Phil, laughing. 'What's wrong with The National?'

'*You* know,' I say. '*You* know. That The National sounds like, umm, a Catholic school boy discovering atheism? Like... pretending not to cry during Robin Williams' speech in *Good Will Hunting*?'

'I liked *Good Will Hunting*!'

'But you know what I mean? How The National sounds like awareness-raising for the stats on male suicide?' I pause. 'Too far?'

'No, I hear it.' Phil swirls his wine, all moody resignation. 'The National sounds like a Polaroid of your pilgrimage to Hemingway's cabin.'

This is why I love Phil.

'But I do still like The National.'

'That's okay,' I tell him. 'You're bisexual. It's not the same.'

October is ending. We want to throw a party that is sort of a Halloween party but is mostly a party for no reason, and so we hose down the plastic lawn chairs and make rice paper rolls and buy two boxes of Banrock wine: goon, but fancy goon. Phil and I go as Thelma and Louise, but our friends assume we're cowboys. Everyone turns up late, dumping their bags on the bed in the spare room. Archimedes is chill but he begs for party pies and then throws up in a potted peace lily.

'Can't wait till Allen moves out,' Phil says dramatically.

'Who's Allen?' say four people.

We explain. Allen's kind of a slimeball. He describes himself as 'a gentleman'. He thinks all his exes are psycho.

'But is he good in bed?' asks Jolene, who is dressed as Ginger Spice.

'He's afraid of cunnilingus. But his family is rich. He has an excellent credit score.'

'Does he have a type?'

'Girls who wear feathered headdresses to music festivals.'

'I think he's my boss,' says Richelle, who 'works in sales' for Billabong, which I recently realised is different to working in retail. 'Does he talk about business getting "actualised"? But he also talks about the time he got "enlightened" on ayahuasca?'

Phil finds this very funny. 'Actually,' he says. 'In that case, I work with a floor full of Allens.'

'Jesus,' says Jolene. 'Keep me on the dole.' But later in the night she says she got offered a bit part on *Neighbours*, so it's hard to feel sorry for her.

In the morning there's a scattering of bodies on the sofas, the spare bed. I collect glasses and dead bottles in a fugue state while Jolene makes coffee. We discover the dishwasher is broken and do the cups by hand. Phil emerges at noon, looking like his eyes have been sewn shut.

'I forgot to tell you,' I say. 'Allen told me you were going to vacuum the floors tomorrow. On account of how my parents are coming to stay next weekend and on account of how I did them last month.'

There's a fraction of a second where Phil's face gets all closed-off and contrarian. But he catches himself. 'I wish I knew when Allen was going to reach adulthood, you know?'

In the afternoon, when everyone is gone, we smoke the rest of a joint that Jolene left on the windowsill, which softens the hangover and has the effect of making our clean apartment seem miraculous and beautiful. I take a shower and Phil sits in the empty bath to keep me company, but my brain fogs over and

I can't keep the thread of our conversation, and when I tune back in Phil is singing a made-up song.

'I need to be different,' I tell Phil, tearful, as he folds me into bed.

'What?' he says. He touches my forehead, like I'm feverish. 'What do you need?'

All I know is there's a terrible wrongness sitting on my chest, mute and heavy like a stubborn cat. This happens sometimes. When I was in high school I would feel it the night before exams, as though the test had already happened and I was sitting with the uncorrectable idiocy of my mistakes, and nothing, not even doing the test, would set things right. It feels like having a spyglass that looks directly into the moment of my death, and the me that is still me is trapped in a terrible puckered face with bad-smelling dentures and I know I have frittered away my entire life. But I can't say that. Instead I say, 'My hair is still wet.' Phil doesn't catch this.

'Other people need to be different,' he says. 'Not us.'

A week goes by. Mondays are awful in the world of adult jobs, but so are Tuesdays, and also the other days. We drink wine and watch Netflix when we eat dinner, and we try not to annoy each other about the dishes, and somehow things stay clean enough. But on Thursday Archimedes goes missing. I am inconsolable. We stand on the road in the early evening and yell down street alleys.

'Meedy! Sir Archimedes Snufflepaw! Come home and we'll feed you peanut butter every day! Meedy!'

Phil walks me home with his arm around me. I chew a hangnail with Terminator-focus.

'He'll turn up,' says Phil. 'He's a collie. They're the cleverest kind.'

82

'And the bravest,' I say.

'Yeah. Meedy's real brave and smart. I bet he had to go save someone, you know? Or solve a crime. He's way more competent than we are. He's probably busting up a drug smuggling ring as we speak.'

My parents turn up with their suitcases that evening. My mother strokes my hair while I lay on the sofa. 'Did you leave the back gate open?' she asks, both sympathetically and unhelpfully.

Phil walks into the room holding a teapot. The carpet is very clean. 'We're blaming Allen,' he says.

'Who's Allen?' says Dad.

'Our dropkick housemate,' says Phil, glancing at me. I shoot him my dagger-eyes. I don't want to play Allen. I just want my dog back.

'Here,' says Mum. 'I'll rustle up some food for us. We'll call the shelter in the morning.'

But Archimedes is not at the shelter. Phil draws up a classy-looking MISSING poster in Illustrator and prints off a ream at work the next day, and in the evening my mother and I wander round the neighbourhood, stapling Meedy's sweet face to telegraph poles. Mum pats me periodically, like I'm the dog. I aim for a brisk, no-nonsense smile, but my eyes keep watering. 'He'll turn up,' says Mum. She gives me a long look. 'You know there's always a space for you back home, don't you, if things don't work out here?'

'I thought you liked Phil!' I say.

'We do, we do. We just...' She trails off, staring up at a pair of sneakers strung over a power line. 'We worry sometimes.'

'We're doing fine for ourselves,' I say. She frowns at my tone. 'My job's fine. Phil's job is very stable and the management is actually very chill. He's really committed. Last week we bought a Nutribullet.'

'Sometimes kids move out of home for a few years,' she says, carefully. 'And then, for whatever reasons, they need to move back for a period of time. And that's okay. I just want you to know you're always welcome back home.'

I punch the stapler to a telegraph pole with both hands. 'Christ, Mum.'

The weekend is meant to be Quality Family Time. My parents came all the way from Adelaide. We go to yum cha, the Opera House. I keep thinking about Meedy throwing up party pies and how I never followed through on my promise to take him to the dog park. Sunday night I am making in-person enquiries at the local shelters when really I should be driving Mum and Dad to the airport, and Phil has an improv thing so he won't be back till nine. Mum tells me not to worry, they'll manage. She leaves me at PAWS FOR THOUGHT ANIMAL HOME and goes to meet Dad back at the house and collect their luggage.

'Let me know, alright, sweetie? When he turns up?'

When I get home it's ten p.m. and the lights are off. The National's 'Don't Swallow the Cap' is blaring through the Bluetooth speaker. 'Phil?' I say. I switch the lights on and the speaker off. The place is empty, but the dishwasher makes a little 'ta-da' noise like it has a surprise for me, and it does, it's working. I tug it open and steam billows out, the dishes pristine. Dad must have fixed it. Actually the whole place looks much cleaner. I imagine my mother scrambling to pack her suitcase and vacuum at the same time and I can't decide who I'm more pissed at: Mum, or Phil, or myself. In the corner of the bedroom, the dog bed has been shaken clean of fur. I run a bath and practise holding my breath for as long as I can, peering up through the floating black curtain of my hair.

On Flexi Friday, cutting through Hyde Park after work, I see Archimedes on a stranger's leash. He's distinctive, for a border collie: dusty brown patches instead of black, pale-blue eyes. 'Archimedes!' I shout.

Meedy looks up, barks happily.

'Hey!' I yell at the stranger, lengthening my stride. He's at least a hundred feet away, heading for the edge of the park. There's a fountain and then some trees between us. It's a warm spring day and several people turn to look at me, even people with earphones. 'Hey, dognapper!' My heels sink into the grass and I kick them off. 'Hey! Dog thief! Stop that guy!'

The stranger cocks his head like someone is calling him from the opposite direction. He steps onto the footpath and turns onto Elizabeth Street.

I run through the park calling, 'Meedy! Meedy!' I can see the back of this guy's head, his dumb grey baker-boy cap disappearing into a wave of pedestrians crossing the street. I weave through the trees. By the time I reach the park's stone gate, they're gone.

'You alright, miss?' A cop in a fluoro vest and bicycle helmet is right there, lounging against the gate. He looks ridiculous, the way cops on bikes do.

'That guy, who just left? He stole my dog!'

I explain the situation, still panting. I can't describe the guy: a white male in a baker's cap. I spend a while describing what I mean by 'baker's cap'. I never saw his face.

'Did other people in the park witness the incident?'

'Incident?'

The cop speaks loudly, like I'm elderly or deaf. 'The gentleman stole your dog.'

'No – oh, that was a week ago. He didn't steal it from me just now. He went up that street.'

'So you saw a man you didn't recognise walking a dog that looked like your dog.'

'If you go now, I bet you could still reach him on your bike.'

The cop regards me coldly. 'Don't have my bike with me just now, I'm afraid.'

I stare up at his helmet. He stares down at my stockinged feet. I stalk off without another word. My shoes are where I left them, tipped over in the grass like two blackout drunks.

Phil finds me at home, face-down on the bed. I relay the story numbly. 'But you're sure it was Meedy?'

'I think I'd recognise my own son.'

'You're cute,' he says.

I flop onto my back. 'He looked happy, too. He looked like he was having a really nice walk. He didn't need us.' My phone rings. 'Will you get that? I'm not done here.'

'Hello?' Phil passes the phone to me, mouths, 'It's your mum.'

'You alright, sweetie?' she says. Her voice is too high and sweet. I feel like a toddler.

'I'm fine.'

'You find Archimedes?'

'Yes,' I say. 'He's doing great.'

'Oh, thank goodness. Well, I was just calling to give you my love, and to say we loved seeing you *and* Phil, and we're very proud of you, okay?'

'Thanks Mum.'

'And please pass on our thanks to Allen for letting us stay in his room. It was very neat. We were a bit flustered, heading out, so we didn't quite catch him. I hope he wasn't offended.'

I sit up. 'Allen?'

'We thought that must have been him in the shower when we left. I heard the water running.'

'Mum, you slept in the spare room. Phil was joking about having a housemate. It's just us two.'

There's a long pause on the other end of the line. Phil is giving me question mark eyebrows. I can hear Dad's gruff voice in the background. 'Must have been Phil home early,' he says.

'Was Phil home early?' asks Mum.

I cover the phone. 'Did you swing home Sunday evening, before Mum and Dad left?' Phil squints.

'Are you okay, Liz?' Mum sounds breathless. 'What's happening?'

'Yeah, Mum,' I say, uncovering the speaker. 'It was just Phil, home early. He didn't realise you guys were still here. Glad you got back safe.'

I hang up.

'You alright?' asks Phil.

'You weren't home early,' I say. I stand and crack the bedroom blinds, stare out.

'What?'

'Sunday night. Someone broke into our place. Took a shower.'

'Hold up,' says Phil. He reaches out his arm, brings me back to the bed. 'Slow down.'

'You got home after I did,' I say. 'You went out for drinks after improv. You said the new member was so unfunny you were signing up for memory-editing.'

'Are you sure that was Sunday?' He squints. It's like he's trying to solve a terrible maths problem. 'Can't have been Sunday.'

'It was.'

He snaps his fingers. 'Jolene. You gave Jolene a spare key.'

'So she broke in and took a shower without telling either of us?'

We sit there, holding our elbows. The evening's still bright. Somehow all the bedroom furniture looks too shiny, like props made for a TV show.

'It must have been me,' says Phil. But he looks baffled.

'Let's get out of here,' I say. 'Let's go get drunk.'

We go to The Clare, where one of Phil's workmates has a DJ set. The place is packed with advertising bros. I can almost see the coke wafting from the speakers. I down two gin and tonics and find Melinda, Brian's wife, who explains she has a baggie in her bra, so we go to a stall together and use the lid of the toilet and my expired Dendy Film membership card. I secretly despise Melinda but she is tolerable once we're on coke. Together we watch the guys play pool but it is too slow, we go upstairs to dance but the music is too weird, we go back to the ladies' for another round and the tiles are slick fluorescent white. I befriend a butch woman named Samia at the bathroom sink and start explaining the plot of *The Truth About Cats & Dogs* to her.

'You just have to pretend, or like, in the world of the narrative, I guess, we have to take it for granted that Janeane Garofalo is fugly and undesirable because she's short, but it's a massive imaginative leap to make, you know? And you have to pretend that Uma Thurman is conventionally attractive.'

'The chick from *Pulp Fiction*? She's hot.'

'But she's hot like an alien is hot, you know? She's like a sexy alien?'

'I took some molly, what about you?'

'Coke, do you want some? Hey, Melinda, are you taking a shit or what?'

'I'm good,' says Samia. 'Don't worry about it.'

'She's not even here. God. I've been abandoned again. Samia, I feel like we have a real connection. Fuck. I have to find Phil.' My heart's banging in my throat. 'You know someone stole my dog?'

'Who?' Samia chews her lip. Her eyelashes are so long.

'A guy named Allen stole my dog!' I grab my purse. 'I have to go find Phil!'

It's all smoke and darkness and pink and orange lights on the dance floor. Phil's jumping and ducking with Brian. I grab his hand. 'I need air!'

On the patio Phil bums a cigarette from a leggy drag queen. 'Do you think Brian's queer?'

'I don't have time for this!' I say. 'I have to ask Mum about Allen!'

'Nope, no, no, bad plan.' Phil twists the phone out of my grip. 'Your make-up is everywhere, Liz, you look like a raccoon. Hey, hey come back!'

He follows me down the fire-escape stairs. I hail a cab and we clamber into the backseat. Phil tries to hug me but his t-shirt is soaked through with sweat and I push him away.

'You okay?' His eyes are huge.

'Meedy left us.' I can't explain it, but I can feel it, I know it's true. I'm suspended between oracular calm and a rage I can't name. 'He left us for another life.'

'Liz,' says Phil, but he breaks off, chews his lip. I check to see if I can keep my hand level. The city gushes through the windows and then we slow, we are home.

Inside, Phil locks the door behind us. It's too quiet.

'I can hear the fridge humming,' whispers Phil.

'Why are you whispering?' I whisper back.

'I feel like there's someone here,' he says, in a normal voice. 'Hello? Is anyone in here?'

'Jesus!' I clamp my hands over his mouth. He giggles.

'I'm kidding, I'm kidding.'

The darkness is cloth-thick. Anyone could be here, a whole crowd of people waiting behind the sofas to jump out and say SURPRISE. It is 2.30 a.m. 'Come with me,' I say softly. 'To turn the lights on.'

Phil finds the hall light, then the bedroom, leaning into the room but still holding my hand, same for the spare bedroom. We check behind the couches. 'I'm fine,' I say to the fridge. 'I'm fine, I'm paranoid, I'm fine.' We sit at the tiny half-table in the kitchen with a glass of water each. Phil raises his to eye level and looks through it.

'I'm not Allen,' he says. 'You know that, right?'

I can only stare at him. His eye is big and wobbly through the glass.

'What are we talking about right now?' I say. 'Have you been playing pranks on me?'

His puts the glass down and then he laughs. 'Oh, god,' he says. 'No. Liz, of course not.'

My shoulders feel like they're trying to hug my ears. Phil folds his arms on the table and plants his forehead between them.

'It was me,' he mumbles into the table. It takes me a minute to hear him. 'I left the gate open. That Thursday when I left for work. That's how Meedy escaped.'

'It's your fault?'

He nods.

I push my chair back. The air is too bright and the glass of the windows is so dark. It's like being inside a lightbulb. 'I need to shower,' I say.

'Liz,' he says. 'Liz, I'm so sorry, please forgive me.'

The bathroom is cool and dark and quiet. I shower with the lights off and sit on the tiled floor and fume. The sobs take me over suddenly, like I'm in shock, but I'm not in shock. Meedy is gone and it is Phil's fault, and this is awful, but I am not surprised, and this is a second awfulness, how not surprised I am. Relationships have costs, Mum says, and you have to decide what you are happy paying, what you are willing to tolerate. I don't want to be furious with Phil. I don't want to lose him on top of Meedy.

I leave the shower and walk into the kitchen streaming water all over the lino. Phil is hunched at the sink, submerged to his elbows, soap bubbles twinkling. I wrap my arms around him, pressing my chest into his back. 'Leave it,' I say. 'Come to bed.'

'I'm useless.' His voice catches. 'You've been doing everything.'

'I haven't,' I tell him. 'You've been stepping up. I've noticed.'

'No,' he says. 'I haven't.'

I look over his shoulder at the window above the sink, meet his eyes in the glass. Behind us are the shadows of the kitchen furniture. A water droplet snakes down my back like a shudder.

'Leave it,' I say, firmly this time. 'Please.'

He lets me lead him to our room. I climb into bed, still damp, turning the sheets cool and clammy. Phil shucks his clothing, turns the light out. My body is jangly, percussive. Some other self will think all this through tomorrow, feel everything tomorrow, take action tomorrow. I'll get up at nine, even if I have a hangover. I'll visit all the animal shelters again and knock on all the doors along our street. Somehow, I'll find our dog. I drift into a half sleep and wake with a jerk, feeling like I'm falling through the air, again and again. Down the hall there is the clanging of pots, the squeak of the tap, water splashing. Phil's arm is warm and heavy on my ribs. Something is wrong, some new thought is waltzing towards me slowly and elegantly. I sit up and listen. Nothing. At last, I discern the near-silent drone of the fridge. It hums on and on, busily cooling its occupants, the jam jars and olive jars and withered celery resting snug in its belly. It's so steady and quiet, I might never notice it again.

Subscribe Now
And receive each issue of HEAT
Australia's international literary magazine

Since its inception in 1996, HEAT has been renowned for a dedication to quality
and a commitment to publishing innovative and imaginative poetry, fiction,
essays, criticism and hybrid forms. Now, in the third series, we are excited to
bring together a selection of the most interesting and adventurous Australian
and overseas writers. HEAT Series 3 is posted to subscribers every two months,
forming a unique, cohesive whole. Your subscription supports independent
literary publishing and enables us to cultivate and champion new and
challenging writing.

Visit giramondopublishing.com/heat/ to subscribe.

The Novel Prize 2022
Entries are now open for The Novel Prize, a biennial award for a book-length
work of literary fiction written in English by published and unpublished
writers around the world. The prize recognises works which explore and
expand the possibilities of the form, and are innovative and imaginative in
style. It offers US$10,000 to the winner and simultaneous publication by
Giramondo Publishing in Australia and New Zealand, by Fitzcarraldo Editions
in the United Kingdom and Ireland, and by New Directions in North America.
Cold Enough for Snow by Jessica Au, the inaugural winner, was unanimously
chosen from over 1,500 entries. It is available now in English and forthcoming
in sixteen languages around the world.

Visit thenovelprize.com for more information. Submissions close 1 June.

Fitzcarraldo Editions

Acknowledgements
We respectfully acknowledge the Gadigal, Burramattagal and Cammeraygal peoples, the traditional owners of the lands where Giramondo's offices are located. We extend our respects to their ancestors and to all First Nations peoples and Elders.

HEAT Series 3 Number 2 has been prepared in collaboration with Ligare Book Printers, Avon Graphics, Ball & Doggett paper suppliers and Candida Stationery – we thank them for their support.

The Giramondo Publishing Company is grateful for the support of Western Sydney University in the implementation of its book publishing program.

Giramondo Publishing is assisted by the Australian Government through the Australia Council for the Arts.

HEAT Series 3
Editor Alexandra Christie
Designer Jenny Grigg
Typesetter Andrew Davies
Digital Producer Alice Desmond
Copy Editor Aleesha Paz
Marketing and Publicity Manager Kate Prendergast
Publishers Ivor Indyk and Evelyn Juers
Associate Publisher Nick Tapper

Editorial Advisory Board
Chris Andrews, Mieke Chew, J.M. Coetzee, Lucy Dougan, Lisa Gorton,
Bella Li, Tamara Sampey-Jawad, Suneeta Peres da Costa,
Alexis Wright and Ashleigh Young.

Contact
For editorial enquiries, please email
heat.editor@giramondopublishing.com.
Follow us on Instagram @HEAT.lit and
Twitter @HEAT_journal.

Accessibility
We understand that some formats will not be accessible to all readers.
If you are a reader with specific access requirements, please contact
orders@giramondopublishing.com.

For more information, visit giramondopublishing.com/heat.

Published April 2022
from the Writing and Society Research Centre
at Western Sydney University
by the Giramondo Publishing Company
PO Box 752
Artarmon NSW 1570 Australia
www.giramondopublishing.com

This collection © Giramondo Publishing 2022
Typeset in Tiempos and Founders Grotesk Condensed
designed by Kris Sowersby at Klim Type Foundry

Printed and bound by Ligare Book Printers
Distributed in Australia by NewSouth Books

A catalogue record for this book is available from
the National Library of Australia.

HEAT Series 3 Number 2
ISBN: 978-1-922725-01-1
ISSN: 1326-1460

ISBN 978-1-922725-01-1

9 781922 725011 >